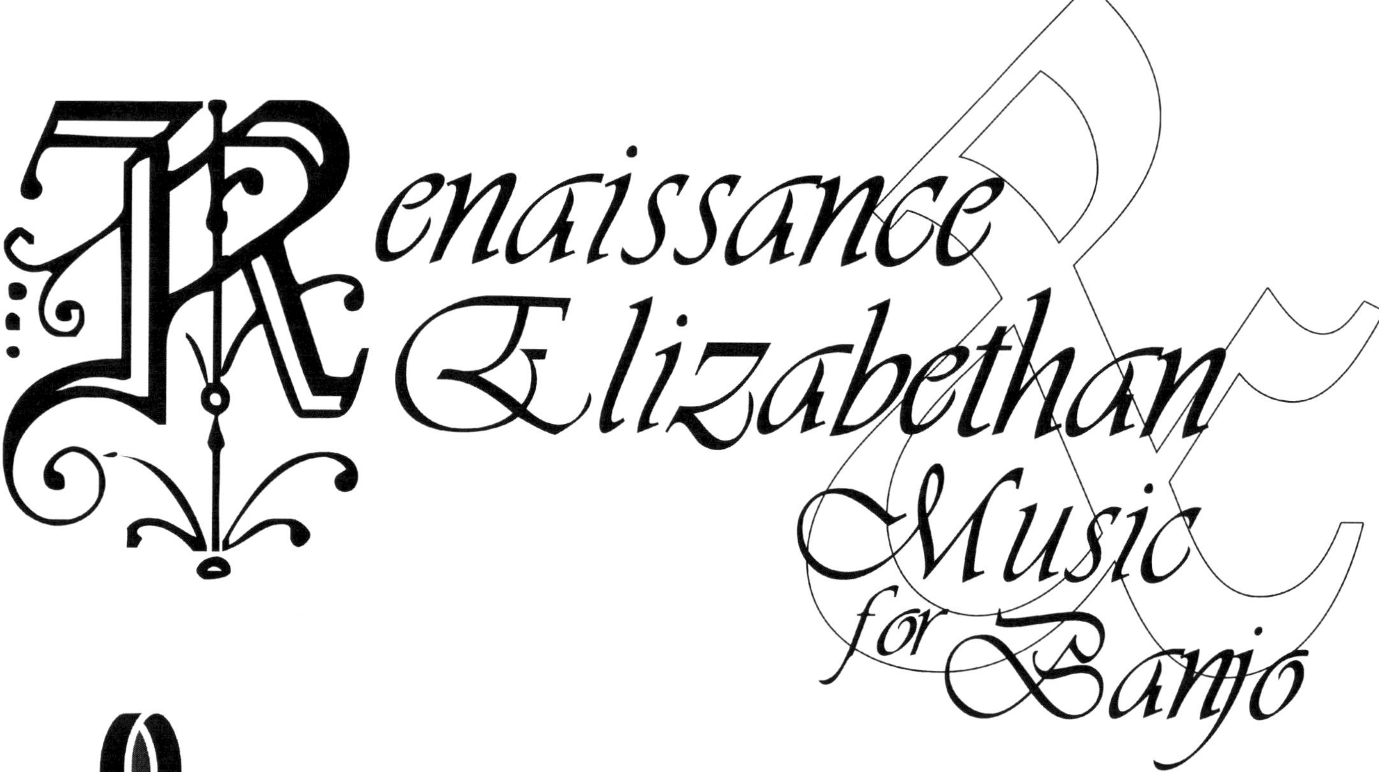

by Kyle Datesman

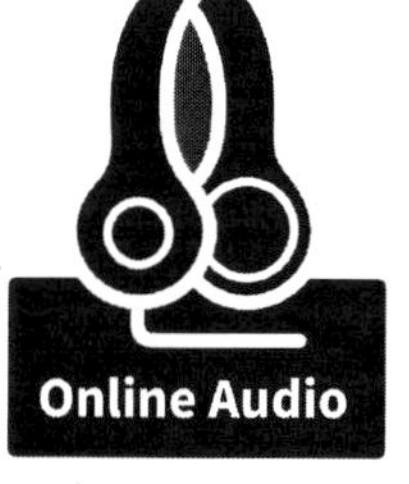

www.melbay.com/96573BCDEB

Audio Contents

1 Greensleeves (chordal)
2 Greensleeves (melodic)
3 What If, A Day, A Month, A Year (chordal)
4 What If, A Day, A Month, A Year (melodic)
5 Lute Lesson (melodic)
6 A Pavane (chordal)
7 Ladies Delight (chordal)
8 Go From My Window (chordal)
9 Queen's Jig (chordal)
10 Queen's Jig (melodic)
11 Shall I Come Sweet Love To Thee (chordal)
12 Come Again (melodic)
13 Lachrimae Pavane (chordal)
14 Lachrimae Pavane (melodic)
15 A Pavane (chordal)
16 A Pavane (melodic)
17 A Ballet (chordal)
18 A Ballet (melodic)
19 Melancholy Galliarde (chordal)
20 A Galliarde (chordal)
21 Tutte Venite Armati (chordal and melodic)
22 Gagliarda Nova (chordal)
23 Gagliarda Nova (melodic)
24 Fantasia (chordal)
25 Villanela (chordal)
26 Villanela (melodic)
27 Gagliarda #2 (chordal)
28 Pavaniglia #2 (chordal)
29 Gagliarda #2 (melodic)
30 Pavaniglia #2 (melodic)
31 Gagliarda #1 (melodic)
32 Pavaniglia #1 (melodic)
33 Spagnoletta (chordal)
34 Spagnoletta (melodic)
35 Guardame Las Vacas (melodic)
36 Sonnett (chordal)
37 Sonnett (melodic)
38 Belle qui tiens ma Vie (chordal)
39 Belle qui tiens ma Vie (melodic)
40 A Galliarde (chordal)
41 A Galliarde (melodic)
42 Etwas Corenten (chordal)
43 Etwas Corenten (melodic)
44 Volte (melodic)
45 Nederlandische Tanz (melodic)
46 Ein Tanz (chordal)
47 Ein Tanz (melodic)

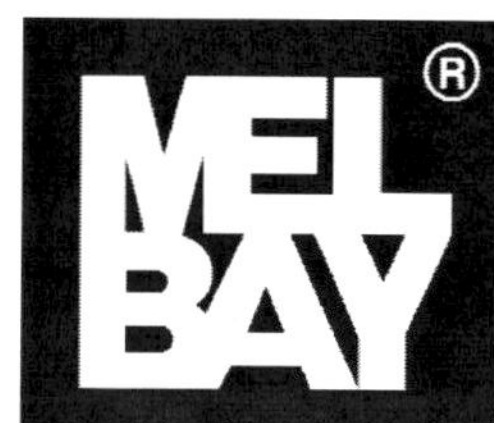

Visit us at www.melbay.com — E-mail us at email@melbay.com

ABOUT THE AUTHOR

Kyle R. Datesman has been playing banjo for over 30 years. After being thoroughly enchanted by the music of lutenist Jan Akkerman he gradually became obsessed with Renaissance lute music. He purchased a lute and tuned it similar to a 5 string banjo, thus making the "connection." During the 1980s, he arranged hundreds upon hundreds of Renaissance, Baroque, Classical, and Celtic pieces for the banjo. He performs at restaurants, Renaissance Faires, weddings, etc. – most anywhere where there is a coin to be caught.

Mr. Datesman holds a Master's degree in Comparative World History from East Stroudsburg University. The 1970s saw him concentrating on the History of Music where in the 1980s he did extensive research into the History of Early Firearms which has become his forte. In the 1990s he was studying first the History of Philosophy and then the Philosophy of History.

He does special exhibits, on the "History of Early Firearms 1320s-1700", for museums, universities, historic sites, etc. The exhibits are comprised of reconstructions which he has built, some from the sketches of Leonardo da Vinci. During 1993 and 1994 he built what some believe to be the world's first, first bicycle, from a da Vinci manuscript which coincidentally is dated to the years 1493 or 1494. His collection was on exhibit in 1992 at the Smithsonian Institute. It was in conjunction with the "Imperial Austria: Art, Arms, and Armor from the state of Styria" exhibit, which is the largest arms and armor collection in the world. It was the first time it was on exhibit outside of Europe.

Spending much of his time moving mountains and wrestling rivers, he subsists in a "hobgoblin's hut" on the banks of Pocono Creek in the beautiful Pocono mountains of Pennsylvania. Does not do well in captivity.

CONTENTS

ELIZABETHAN - (1550s-1610s)

CONTINENTAL RENAISSANCE - (1450s - 1590s)

INTRODUCTION

On many a sheet-music-seeking pilgrimage the author, rummaging around in the banjo bin, became acutely aware of the lack of "growing material." Where "How To" instructional-type books were aplenty, collections of more advanced pieces were rather hard to find. What is more, although it certainly is not the case, it appeared that the banjo repertoire was exhausted. How many more arrangements of "Cripple Creek," "John Hardy," "Joe Clark," etc. do we really need? The 5-string deserves better. This book was written as a response to this stagnation.

Another reason for this undertaking was the interesting connection between the banjo players and musicians at various "Renaissance Faires." While working at these Faires, the author has met a number of "closet" banjo players, masquerading as troubadours playing citterns, lutes, mandolas, etc. The musicians are "former" bluegrass players who have retuned their medieval instruments to a tuning they feel comfortable with — standard banjo tuning. They then are able to play the traditional Anglo-Celtic fiddle tunes that they originally were trained to play on the banjo. This also makes it much easier for them to learn new Celtic pieces. Learning more appropriate Renaissance pieces seemed to pose more of a problem for them as these tunes are usually a bit more complicated. To learn such music without written notation would prove to be very difficult. A light bulb made an appearance and a few years later a need was met.

During the 1980s when these tablatures were arranged, banjo players and bluegrass musicians in general appeared to want to break away from the hillbilly image, experiment with other types of music and expand into other areas. Music which still retained some bluegrass characteristics was referred to as "New Grass" while those that threw out the baby with the bathwater started making arrangements of Bach, Beethoven and the Beatles. Some artists, such as David Grisman, created a form he believed warranted a new category entirely and labeled it "Dawg Music."

Grisman's music brings to light an interesting concept. Wanting to project a more sophisticated image, he retained instruments which have a history of sophisticated associations. The guitar has its collection of virtuosos under the patriarch Segovia. The mandolin reeks of Renaissance Italy and even Vivaldi wrote for it. The bass fiddle could be seen as a bass violin and in the credits to Grisman's works the fiddle miraculously metamorphised into a violin. And the banjo... It appears that the banjo had only a mere 20 year stint with art music in the late 19th century — nowhere near enough time to impart an aura of elitism. Not enough time to remove that metallic clankety-clank of garbage can lids being smashed together in some back yard. You can take the banjo out of the country, but... or so it seems.

Used in the context of Grisman's fast paced acoustic jazz, the banjo would still retain the rapid staccato-like rhythm and thus would be a dead giveaway of its peasant origins. This would be a strong bond with bluegrass that Grisman would have like severed. But when played slowly, and utilizing full chords, music results that seems refreshingly foreign to what we expect from the banjo. Thus, the country can be taken from the banjo if one would want to. Or can it? Even though the resulting sounds are a far cry from what, as Americans, we associate as "country," Celtic and Renaissance pieces evoke images of green fields, stone walls, thatched roofs, Alpine lakes and Robin Hood. A "Country sound" of a different sort. Perhaps the term "Old Country" would suffice.

I would suspect that some crusty, old bluegrass "purist" might take exception to learning a lick from snotty "high-brow" music — a case of reverse snobbery. For this there is no need as it may come as a surprise to many "purists," 3-fingered banjo picking was originally used by banjoists playing classical music during the 1880s and 1890s. Classical banjo was an urban phenomenon at this time, and led directly to the development of bluegrass banjo technique.

In effect, classical banjo is more "traditional" than bluegrass in a chronological time frame. Thus, being kissing cousins, Scruggs and Scarlotti, Munde and Mozart, Dillard and Dowland all have more in common than some would like to admit. There should be no qualms about bluegrass banjoists playing this music. The tunes do not even have to be an end in themselves. They can be viewed and used as a means to overall better banjo playing. The left hand will adapt to new and unusual fingering while the right hand will discover refreshing rolls and melodic runs it never knew existed — all without having to retune the instrument. Your hand will become more dexterous and your bluegrass playing will become more advanced. Although these tablatures are intended to be played and appreciated for their own sake, there will be those who insist on treating them as "limbering up" exercises for their bluegrass playing - - an interesting and refreshing twist on the attitude that violinists have for fiddle tunes.

Kyle R. Datesman

PREFACE

The tablatures in this book present music which is very foreign to the 5-string banjo. Designed to be played much, much slower than the tempos bluegrass musicians are used to, it incorporates many rests, pinches and full chordal strums. Arpeggios are found but much less so then in "roll-oriented" bluegrass banjo.

Many notes will be sounded simultaneously – a rather unfamiliar concept to the bluegrass banjoist. This means an antithesis to the dogma in bluegrass playing that the same finger is never used in succession. This "rule" is what allows for the incredible breakneck speeds often found in bluegrass music. But it is necessary to dispense with this philosophy if one is to play "Renaissance banjo." This is especially true with the more vertical chordal arrangements. Naturally, this is bound to slow down your playing speed. But this is fine, for if one is to play this music well it would not hurt if the performer has a depression problem. This aids to capture the essence of much of the music and is historically accurate. If one does not have a depression problem he is sure to acquire one after much exposure to this type of music. I don't know how I managed it, but somehow I ended up playing the most depressing music imaginable (Renaissance lute music) and the happiest music imaginable (Bluegrass banjo music). In order for a musician to play any type of music it is advisable that they become familiar with it through listening to performances. This is essential in this instance, due to the the great gaps in style between Bluegrass and Renaissance music. Chronic depression is the risk one must take.

Most of this music is relatively unsophisticated strophic dance music while some is more difficult thorough composed pieces. All are arranged on the popular (at that time) "theme and variations" structure. The tune is presented first in a slow, chordal arrangement and then again in its entirety in a more rapid, linear, perpetual-motion melodic style better suited to the bluegrass banjoist. It has been done this way in order to help the performer make the transition from a style he is familiar with to one he is not.

The tablatures are rather self-explanatory. Time signatures are provided. In some of the pieces, the fifth string should be retuned – this being indicated. Right-hand fingerings are omitted for in this style of music there usually are a number of different ways to finger a given passage. The performer should use whatever fingering feels most comfortable. "Lead-ins" are not provided for this music is intended for the accomplished player and so it is assumed that he would consider them superfluous and improvise. Repeat cadences and endings, likewise, are omitted for much the same reason. In Renaissance music as in Bluegrass, sometimes the last phrase or two is repeated to act as an ending cadence. This adds a nice touch and gives the listener an opportunity to anticipate the end of the piece.

Strophic tunes are usually treated much the same way as Bluegrass breakdowns and fiddle tunes. The first section is repeated before going on to the second, which is then also repeated. How many times this is carried on as well as how many times an ending cadence is repeated is left to the discretion of the performer. Thorough composed pieces are often repeated in their entirety.

Rhythmic interpretation and the peculiarities of phrasing are in the hands of the performer. Most banjo music is pretty straight-forward rhythmically and changes little through the duration of the tune. This is not necessarily so in Renaissance music where the rhythm may vary widely within the framework of a single piece. It may pick up or slow down accordingly. This often is in accord with the mood of the passage, speeding up when optimism is felt and slowing down when depression sets in. This is one of the reasons why Renaissance music should be "experienced" before being attempted to play in order to get the proper feel for it.

On the page preceding every tablature is a short commentary describing the piece. In most books these commentaries center on the individual composers, their lives and their publications. I have tried to avoid this and instead have restricted myself to descriptions of the music itself. This, I feel, is what the performer is more interested in and is of much more use to him.

In order to make full use of these commentaries, it would help if the performer has some knowledge of elementary music theory. It is advisable to know all of the major and minor chords and how they related to each other. In these commentaries I have made references to the pieces as being either in a major or a minor key. This is only half correct. As has been noted, many tunes begin in one "key" and end in another. What key then is the entire piece in? This makes matters very confusing.

What is more, some music theorists would object to applying the terms "major" and "minor" to this style of music. These terms came about only in the 1600s when the modern standard notation and tonality originated. Almost all of the works in this collection date from the 1500s when these terms were not in use. During this time, the scales and tonality in use were referred to as modal, which means they were based on scales dating back to the ancient mid-East. What makes matters even more confusing is that this was the time, 1500s to 1600s, when the transition to the modern scales were made. The same work may show characteristics of both the ancient modal and the modern Major/Minor. I have used the terms "Major" and "Minor" simply as an aid to the bluegrass banjoist to make the situation more easily understood and dispensed with any reference to the ancient modal scales.

In the commentaries, sometimes references are made to a particular measure. The measures are numbered continuously through the entire piece. For instance, the typical dance form of two sections of eight measures each, the first measure of the second section is referred to as measure #9. The numbering does not start again from the beginning of each section. When references are made to the right hand and the left hand, it is assumed that the performer is right handed.

I would like to thank Jim Kirkuff for encouragement, guidance, and advice on the music business. Genuine encouragement and benevolence, I have discovered, is rarely found among academics. There are, however, a few exceptions — Professor Earl Page of Northampton Community College, Professor John Muncie, Professor Neil Hogan and Professor Eshelmann of East Stoudsburg University and Professor Vernard Foley of Purdue University. These men have provided much encouragement and inspiration over the years. More importantly they have shown me benevolence in a world where it is truly lacking.

I would also like to thank the late Carl Datesman, the late Hilda Lahr, mom and dad – especially mom, who constantly hounded me with questions like, "why don't you play your banjo anymore"?, or "you're not selling your banjo are you"? I would like to thank Uncle Donald Lahr, who at picnics and hunting trips, often would approach me and ask, in hushed tones, "Kip, I brought along my guitar, did you bring along your banjo"? I would like to thank Gary Shaeffer and the boys, for being such the great guy he is, Galen Worthen, Frank Cotonzare III, for being the best, best friend that one could ever have, Brian Miller, just for laughs (I just know he is going to get a big kick out of some of the things in this book) and how could we forget Scott Guilds. Finally, I suppose that I should thank a certain special lady, who in her own unique way had everything to do with this undertaking.

Question: Why is there so much music written about unrequited love?

Answer: When love is requited there are better things to do than write music!

GLOSSARY

1. **Anticipation/resolution** - Much of the emotional aspect of music has to do with these two concepts. Most music (impressionism, expressionism, and serialism are the exceptions) begins in a certain key, moves away from it in varying degrees and then usually returns to it at the end. Anticipation is the feeling one gets while waiting for this to happen. Resolution is when it finally does happen.

2. **Arpeggios** - This is what happens when a chord is taken and "drawn out linearly." The notes of the chord are played in succession instead of simultaneously as a chord is usually presented. Much of Scrugg's style of banjo playing is based upon this technique.

3. **Ayre** - A type of song popular in England during the 1590s-1610s period. Pronounced the same, it is not to be confused with another type of song – the "air." It usually was performed by a lute player and a single vocalist. John Dowland was the most famous composer of Ayres and so it should come as no surprise that many were tragic.

4. **Cadence** - An ending; whether for a section, phrase or the entire tune. Usually comprised of 2 to 4 measures.

5. **Consonance** - When two tones are sounded simultaneously and are pleasing to the ear they are said to be consonant. It could be said that "consonance is in the ear of the beholder" for what is considered consonant varies across different cultures. Even in the same culture one can find changes for what may be consonant in one century may not be in the next. Its opposite is "dissonance."

6. **Dance Form -** This should need no introduction to the bluegrass musician as all hoe-downs, breakdowns, and fiddle tunes use this structure. It is strophic in nature and comprised of either 2 or 3 sections of 8 to 10 measures each. They are repeated as often as desired.

7. **Dance Pairs** - It was common in the 15th and early 16th century to take 2 dances and pair them together. Originally it was done with 2 dances which used the same thematic material (identical in melody and harmony) but had different time signatures. The first one usually was played briskly in triple time 3/4 or 6/8, and then the second more slowly in double time 2/4 or 4/4. Thus, a "dance pair" was essentially the same tune repeated in a different time signature.

8. **Dowland, John** - One of the most famous composers of his day and certainly the most well-known lutenist. It was fashionable to be depressed during these times, Dowland being especially noted for it. Semper Dowland, Semper Dolens – Always Dowland, Always Dolcful.

9. **Early Music** - This is a "catch-all" term used to describe European music of the Medieval and Renaissance periods dating from roughly 500 AD to 1600 AD. Sometimes the Baroque period, 1600-1750 is included.

10. **Elizabethan Era** - This is a term used to describe England during the rule of Queen Elizabeth I, who ruled from the 1550s to the first few years of the 1600s. This was the time when England experienced the Renaissance to the fullest and was at the height of its cultural flowering. It provided such notables as Shakespeare, Walter Raleigh, and Francis Drake.

11. **Elizabethan Music** - The music of this cultural flowering. It is characterized as being somewhere between art music and folk music, showing traits of both. It was also a transition period between the ancient modal and the modern major/minor scales and tonality. William Byrd, Thomas Morley and the great John Dowland were its patriarchs. Viols, Lutes, and the Virginal were the fashionable instruments.

12. **Fantasia/Fantasy/Fancy** - A free form. Usually very contrapuntal (polyphonic) and complex, it allowed the composer much artistic license. Often of a surrealistic nature.

13. **Galliarde/Gagliarda** - A very popular dance of the 1500s. It was originally lively and upbeat, sometimes with jumps and skips involved. It was always in triple time and by the 1600s when it became stylized, it also became somewhat doleful. Used as part of a dance pair it preceded the pavane.

14. Hocket - A technique that was popular during the 1300s, especially in England. The notes were syncopated to give a jumpy, staggered quality which sounds very much like the "dotted rhythms" of some hornpipes. It was used primarily during the 1300s but was seen only rarely centuries afterwards.

15. Horizontal/Linear - A style where most of the notes are sounded in succession not simultaneously. A melodic line is produced not chords. Melody results. The term "horizontal" comes from the way it appears when written down; as the successive notes are written one after the other or horizontally. The second rendition of the pieces in this book use this style. The opposite of vertical/chordal.

16. Imitation - A technique which became popular during the 1400s and persisted into the next century. A musical phrase was stated and then it was repeated in either a different octave or in another key. Thus, the musical thought was "imitated." Row, row, row, your boat" is probably the most famous example of this style.

17. Interval - A note is an individual sound; a chord is 3 of these individual sounds sounded simultaneously; an interval is 2 of these individual sounds sounded simultaneously. An interval is between a note and a chord and originated sometime around 700-800 AD.

18. Jig - A lively dance found in Anglo-celtic areas. Strictly speaking a jig is in 6/8 time, but down through the ages some tunes have been wrongly called jigs even though they use a different time signature.

19. Major/Minor scales - During the 1600s some of the old modal scales were combined and altered to create 3 new scales, one major and 2 minors and an entirely new system of music theory. The Lydian and Ionian modes were used to create major scales, while Dorian and Aeolian modes were used for the 2 minor scales. (The minor scale can be considered as 2 scales for it differed when ascending and descending.) The 1600s was a time when faith and superstition gave way to enlightenment and rationalization. This tendency was applied to the music of the times as well. The result was the major/minor tonality, which was a new more rational and standardized system of music theory.

20. Modal - This refers to archaic scales, either Eurasian or other, that existed prior to the innovation of major/minor scales and tonality in the 1600s. They were of quite a variety, some being known as the Ecclesiastical or "church modes." Some of them have survived to this day in folk music of various sorts. During the late 1500s to early 1600s modal scales began to blend in with the newer major/minor tonality and thus it is sometimes hard to determine whether a piece is modal, major, minor, or what.

21. Part or Section - In strophic pieces, a part or section is comprised of 8 to 10 measures. It encompasses an entire comprehensive musical statement as the tension is almost always resolved by the last measure. It usually is made up of 2 phrases which are closely related. 2 or 3 parts or sections are used together to create a strophic song or dance. It is usual to repeat sections perhaps varying it slightly each time.

22. Pavane/Pavin/Pavaniglia - A very popular dance of the 1500s. It was always in duple time and very doleful. Used as part of a dance pair it came after the Galliarde.

23. Perpetual Motion - A style of music where there is a continuous, never-ending stream of notes with very few if any rests to interrupt it. Obviously it is much easier to perform with a linear melodic style instead of a vertical chordal one. Perpetual motion is used in the second rendition of the pieces in this book.

24. Phrase - A musical "thought" or "sentence." Usually made up of 2 to 4 measures-sometimes more.

25. Renaissance - A cultural phenomenon in Europe which occurred during the early 1300s to the early 1500s. What characterized the period was a revival of ancient (Greek and Roman) learning, along with emphasis on humanism and "this world" instead of the "afterworld." It began in Italy and gradually spread to other areas – the British Isles being one of the last places it reached. The word is French and translates as "rebirth," referring to the revival of many aspects of antiquity.

26. Renaissance Music - This term is actually a misnomer. Since the Renaissance was a revival of ancient learning, one would naturally assume that ancient music would be revived as well. This was not the case as it was practically unheard of during the Renaissance and has undergone a revival only during our own times. What it refers to is the music of the Renaissance period which was actually a refinement of Medieval music – the style of music which preceded it. Thus, it has nothing to do with the revival of ancient music and can be a very misleading and confusing term. Most Renaissance music was polyphonic (many-voiced) which means that it was comprised of a number of independent melodic lines, each carrying its own weight, with none dominating the others. They were all woven together to create interesting and sometimes unpleasant harmonies. Homophonic (one-voiced) music was unusual. In this style only one melodic line was emphasized while the others acted in supporting roles. Renaissance music encompasses the period from roughly 1450s to the 1590s. One may notice that this time frame does not coincide exactly with that of "the Renaissance" as a cultural phenomenon, but is slightly later. There are a number of reasons for this and it certainly makes the term "Renaissance music" even more confusing.

27. Resolution - Almost all music except impressionism, expressionism, and serialism is created by building up tension, either suddenly or gradually, and then releasing it. The tension is caused by moving away from the tonic key, and is eventually "resolved" by moving back to it. One can sense whether resolution has occurred or not. Unresolved music has a feeling of incompletion – it sounds as if the tune is left hanging. This is intuitive, for even children are able to tell the difference. It is analogous to a spring, where it is wound up under tension and then released returning back to its original position.

28. Staccato - This is where the same note is repeated in quick succession, which gives the music much the sound of a machine gun.

29. Strophic - This is a term used to describe music which is comprised of a number of sections anywhere from 2 to 4, which are repeated over and over, often varied slightly each time. All bluegrass and folk music fall into this category as well as Renaissance dances and songs. The opposite category is thorough composed pieces.

30. Stylized Dance - Originally dances were meant to be danced to. They were melodically and structurally simple to accommodate this. But by the late 1500s they began to get so complex that to actually dance to them was out of the question. They then became known as "stylized dances." By the early to mid 1600s they were put together in groups comprised of 4 to 5 of these stylized dances which were related only by key. These groups were called "dance suites" and were quite lengthy. Eventually the word "dance" was dropped and they became known simply as "suites", as all evidence of their dance origins was eliminated. Their importance is exemplified by the fact that the symphony of the Classical music era is believed to have evolved from the dance suite.

31. 16th-Note Flurries - Sometimes 8th notes are divided further into faster paced 16th notes. They usually are in sets of 4 or multiples of 4. It was fashionable to rattle off these "flurries" near the end of a piece as a display of ones' virtuosity. Perhaps by the end the performer was confident enough to brave such adventures.

32. Theme and Variations - A popular form during the 1500s. A phrase or two is stated and then repeated repeatedly but each time with slight variations, thus the name. Later thorough composed works may have derived from it.

33. Thorough Composed - A term describing a piece which is not broken up into individual sections but rather is comprised of a very long one. Occasionally it may be repeated in its entirety. The opposite category is strophic pieces.

34. Tonality - Music theory; the theory, rules and laws that lie behind what one hears. The laws of relationship among all of the notes, intervals, and chords. The 1600s saw a new tonality emerge.

35. Tonic or Tone Key - The tonic is the key the piece is in. Either whichever it starts or ends in.

36. Vertical/Chordal - A style where many of the notes are sounded simultaneously, producing intervals and chords. Harmony results. Consonant harmony if we are lucky. The term "vertical" comes from the way it appears when written down, as the simultaneous notes are written one on top of the other or vertically. The first rendition of the pieces in the book use this style. It is the opposite of horizontal/ linear.

37. Villanella - A popular dance in Italy during the 1400s and 1500s. It derived largely from folk music and it is believed that it influenced the later Madrigal.

REPERTOIRE

Greensleeves (English)

Somehow or another it made its way here. It is an often requested tune and thus I cannot ignore it. But I can do things with it; such as present it in 2 different keys. Something must be done to break the monotony. Perhaps its unending popularity has to do with the fact that it is so emotionally versatile. It can be played upbeat or passive – depending on the performers' or the audiences' mood. I understand that since the 16th century many poems about famous executions have been set to it. It is arranged here in E minor and D minor respectively. What more could be said about Greensleeves?

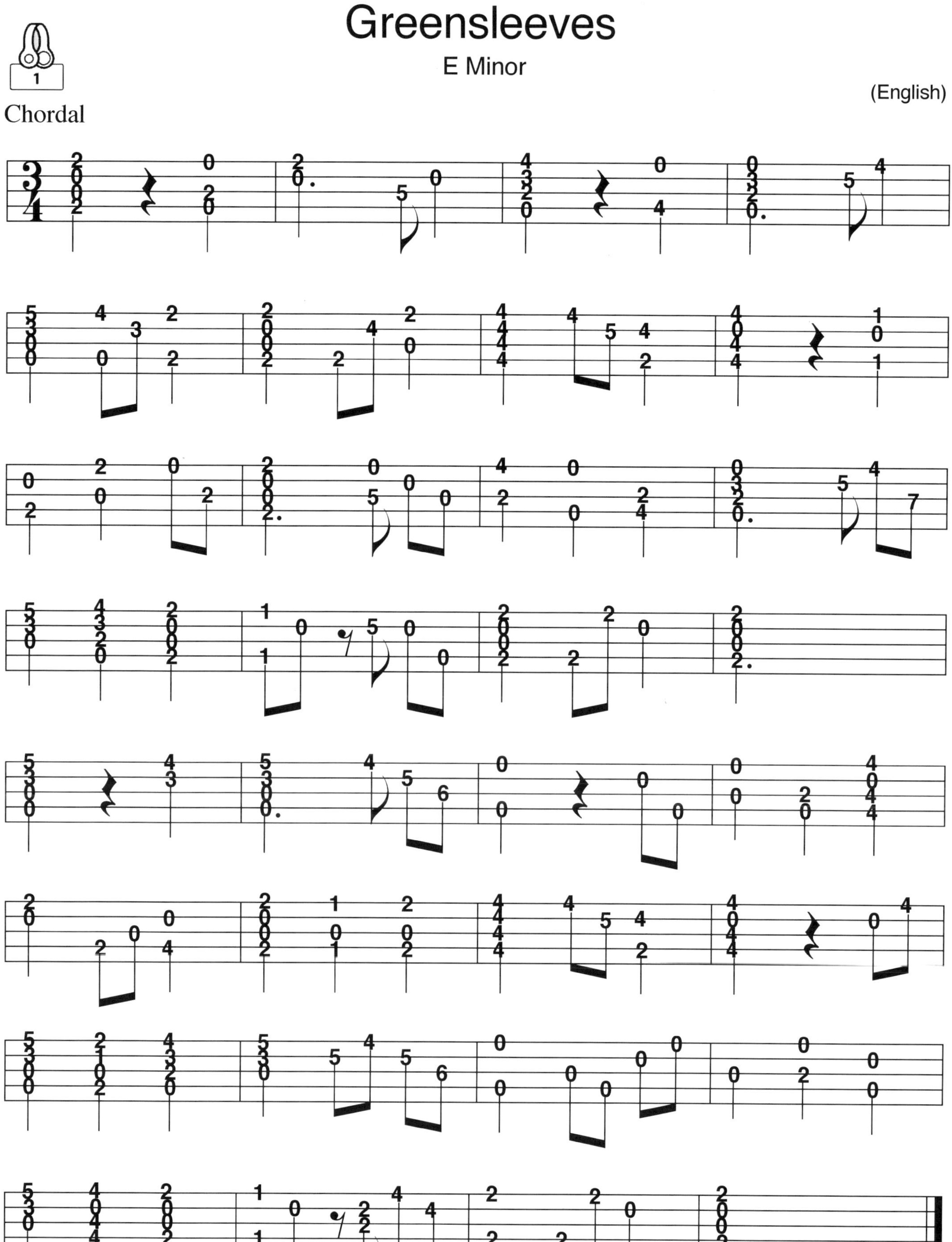
Greensleeves
E Minor
(English)
1
Chordal

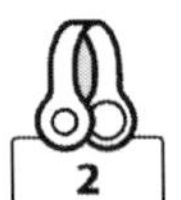

Greensleeves

E Minor

(English)

Melodic

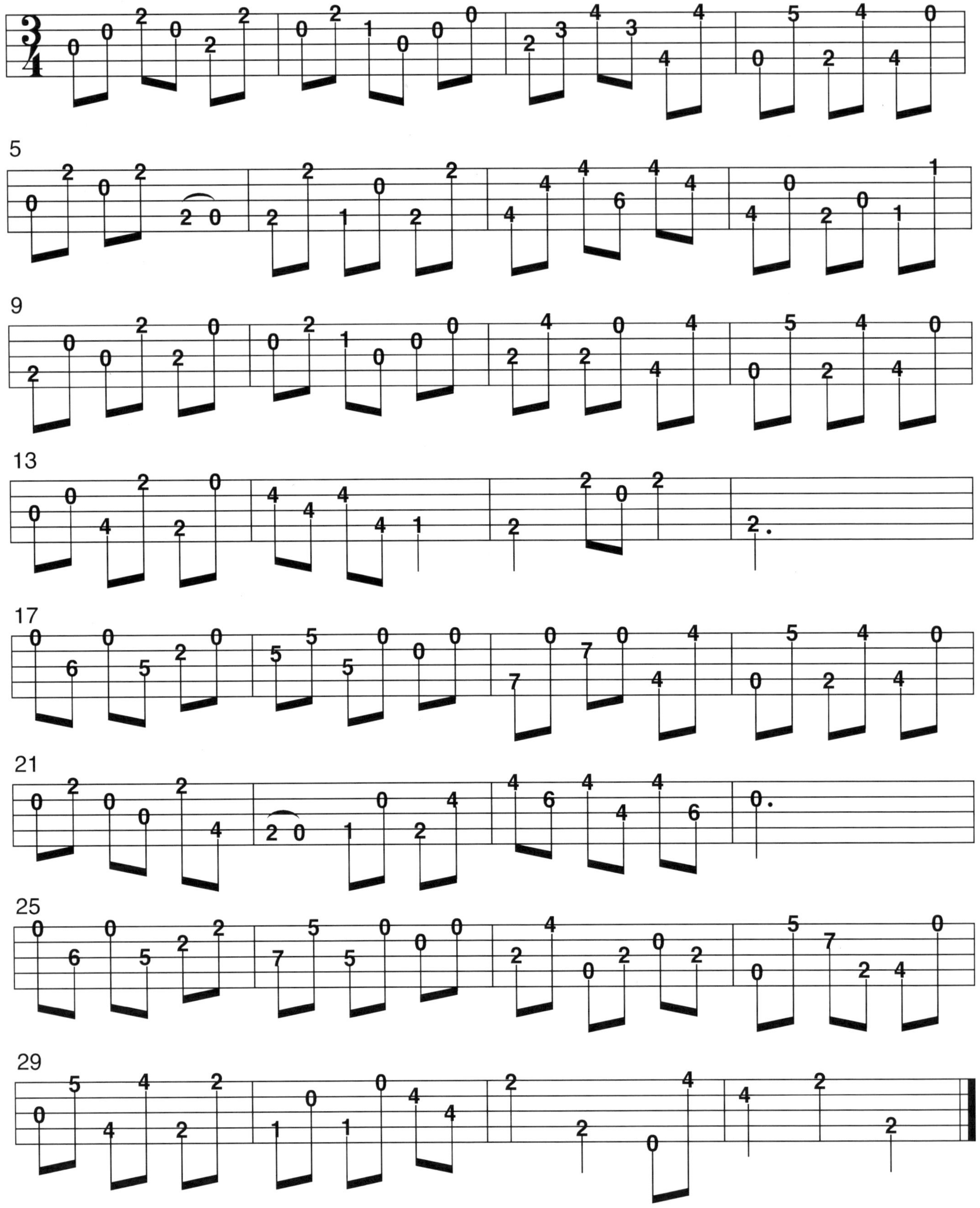

Greensleeves

D Minor

(English)

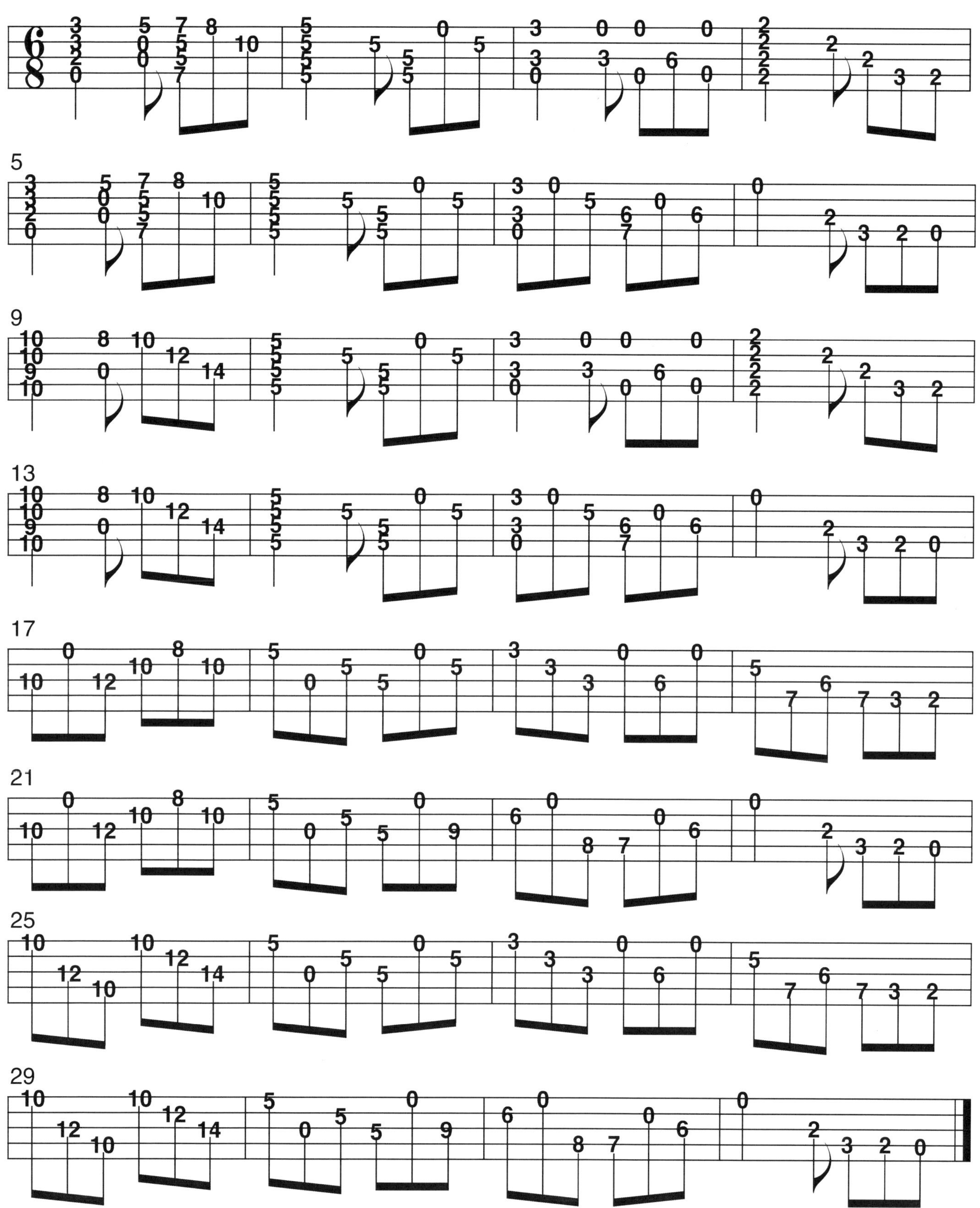

The Willow Song (English)

I learned this piece from a female vocalist at one of the Renaissance Faires I played at. This is a common way to learn new tunes. It apparently was well-liked in its own day as Shakespeare used it in his play "Othello." It is a good example of a late Ayre and as such does not fit exactly into a dance form. It has two sections, the first having 14 measures and the second 8. Typical of Elizabethan lute music, it is of very solemn character.

It begins by stating a melancholy musical thought in the first two measures. This is then reinforced, two measures later, by a similar thought but in a higher register. This serves to acknowledge that the first one was indeed true. The next six measures continue the passive feeling. This is then repeated again in the measures #11-14 as if to drive home the point. The second section has the same quality and feel as the first, and in fact it repeats many of its thoughts and phrases. This is true for much of the tune and lends it a bland monotonous tone, a persistent perpetual depression that ceases not for a moment.

One of the reasons that I like this tune is that it is in a somewhat unusual key – F Major. Unusual for the 5-string banjo at least. Being in F Major, C Major is found consistently. F Major's relative minor, D minor, is in abundance while G Major is somewhat rare. It's relative minor, E minor, is used in the ending cadences resolving into the tone key, F Major. There is a very interesting cadence in measure #9 which employs A Major. This cadence resolves into an A minor in the 10th measure which is a rather unusual occurrence. B♭ Major has its place in a number of instances. G minor shows up in only one spot, measure #15, the first of the second section.

The Willow Song

F Major

(English)

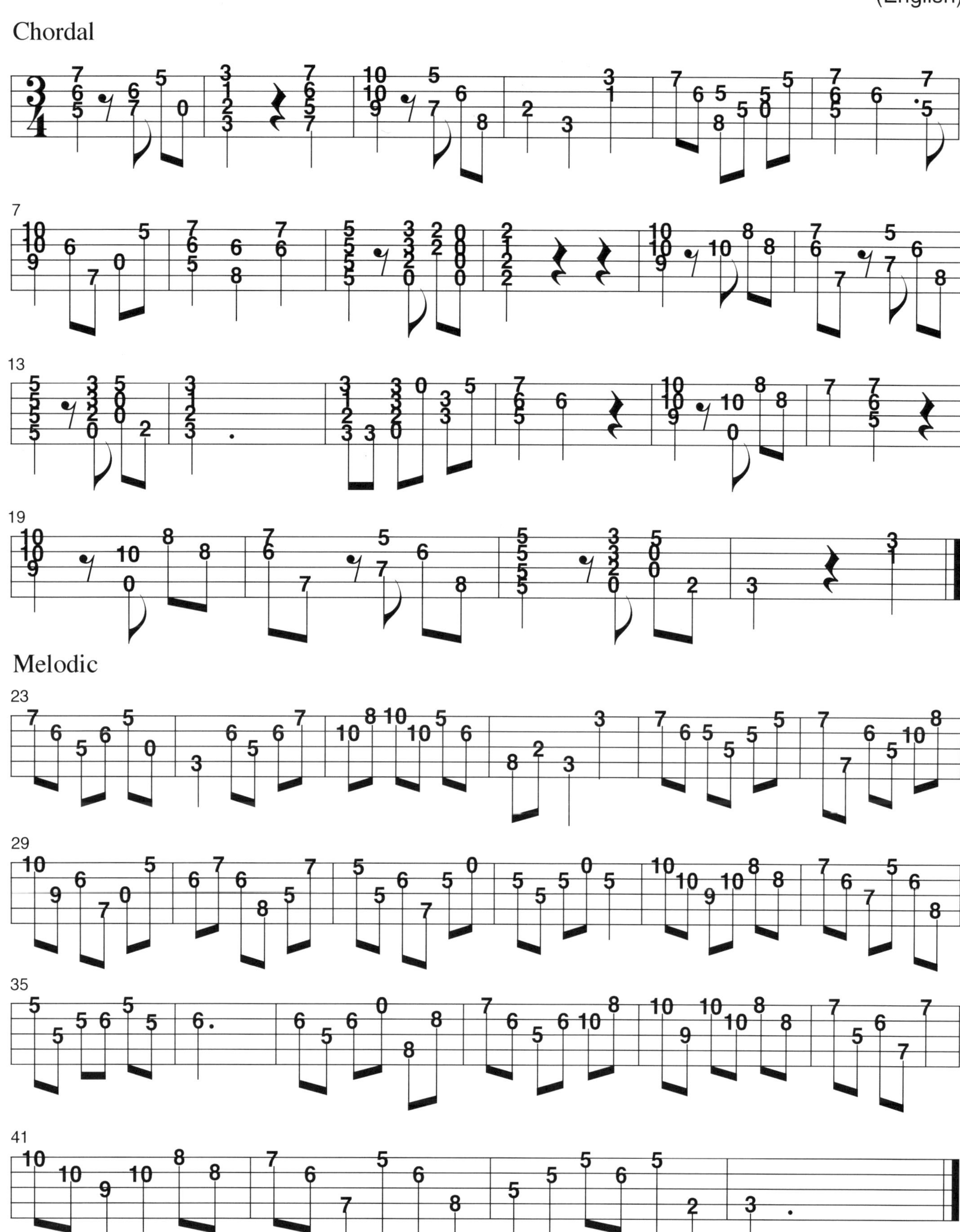

What If, A Day, A Month, A Year (English)

This is another light relatively easy piece which is unsophisticated but yet not completely strophic. Four extra measures had been added to the first part. The feel of the piece at this juncture is that there was more to say than could be said in the usual eight measure time frame. The ascending scale in measure #12, which ends the phrase, suggests enough time was acquired with the additional measures to complete the thought. The rapidly ascending passage, ending on a very high note, gives the feeling of relieved satisfaction that the time quota was met.

The general mood of this tune is that of apprehension. The piece is in A minor and in the first two measures it feels as if it wants to work its way to E Major but has difficulty. A minor reappears in the 3rd measure, but again it is unstable and wants to go somewhere. It tries to go to C Major in measure #4 but is not comfortable there and so again tries its initial attempt to flow into E Major, again with much difficulty. Still not satisfied it uses measures #7-10 to take perhaps another different route to E Major. Happy that it had finally arrived, the jubilant ascending scale ending in measures #11-12 celebrates the accomplishments.

Contentment sets in during the 13th and 14th measures. It is as if the problem of arriving at E Major has been resolved with its effortless transition from C Major to G Major to A minor and then finally to E Major. But doubt and cynicism are expressed in the next two measures of the piece, as it seems to say that perhaps there are many ways to get to E Major and that maybe it is not so important which one is used after all.

The cautionary mood of the work causes one to instinctively pause whenever E Major is arrived at – whether contentedly or not. The first few notes when trying to move to E Major have an upbeat optimistic feel that evaporates when it becomes obvious that the path taken is not the right one. Frustration is then the result and thus the pensive pauses when E Major is met.

The piece is in A minor, but the target of many of the musical ventures is E Major. C Major is used quite often. E minor and B minor are used in measures #15-16 when expressing cynicism and doubt. G Major is used here in a transitional mode when moving from one chord to another.

What If, A Day, A Month, A Year

A Major

(English)

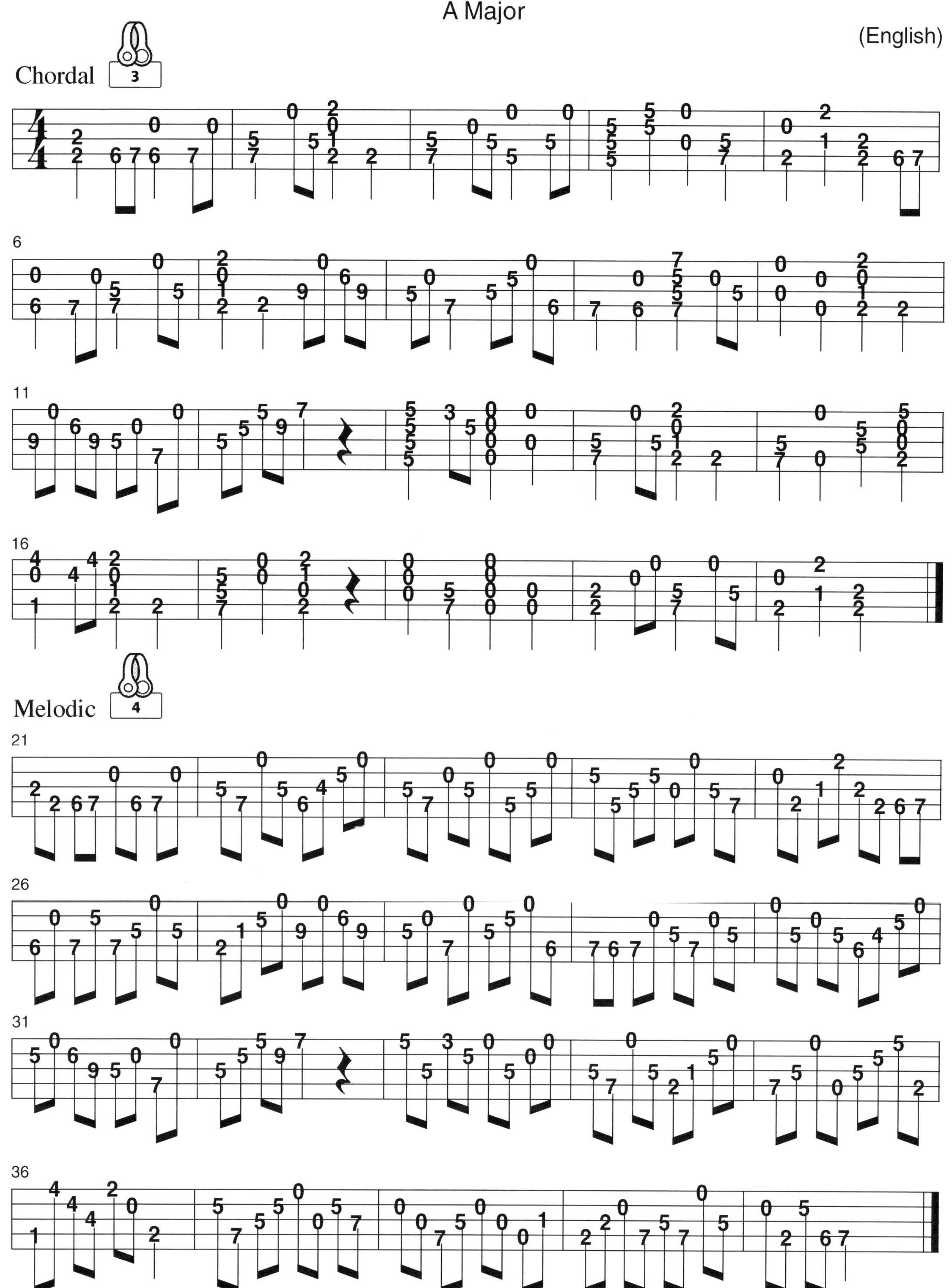

The Ladies Delight (English)

This tune was included in this collection for it is a piece in 6/8 time, yet is not a jig. It is in G Major using C Major and D Major extensively. Notwithstanding its apparent simplicity the work shows some interesting characteristics. Sometimes D Major, which is what is usually used when resolving to the tonic key, is replaced by F Major. This gives it a quavering transitory quality and a feeling of uncertainty. The concept of imitation is hinted at for the phrase in measure #9 is again repeated in C Major in the following measure and in D Major in measure #12. E minor, the relative minor of the tonic key makes a rare appearance in the 14th measure as part of a descending phrase. The phrase winds down from G Major to F Major in measure #13, then to E Minor and D Major in the following measure, to C Major and again D Major in the 15th measure and then finally resolves to G Major. The last eight measures of the piece is a variation of measures #9-16.

This tune asks for you to pick up the tempo. The perpetual motion version seems as if it will never come to an end. Although the tune is very upbeat, resolution comes slow and one is kept in a state of unbearable musical anticipation.

The Ladies Delight

G Major

(English)

Chordal

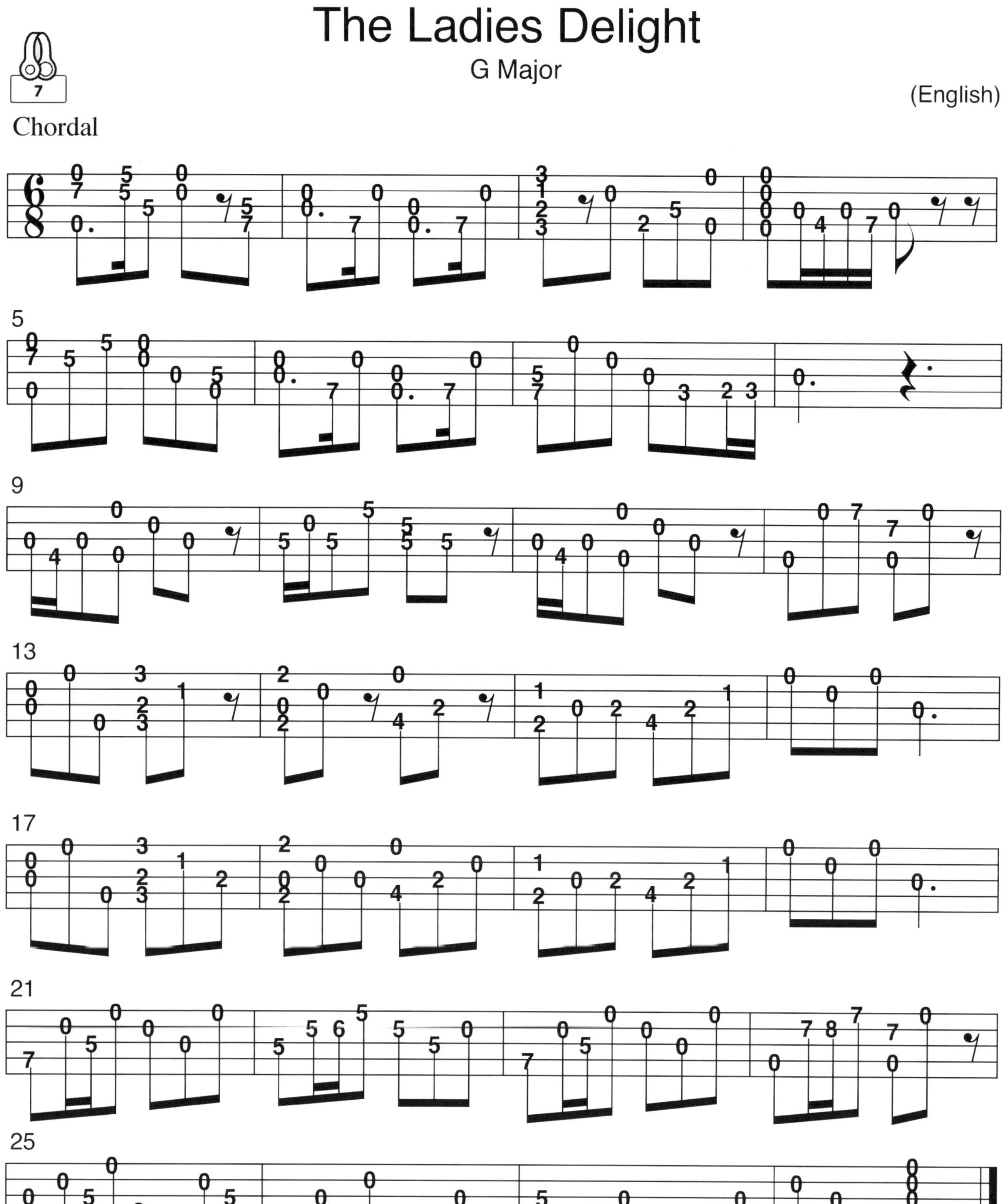

The Ladies Delight

G Major

(English)

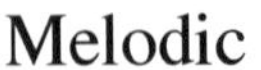

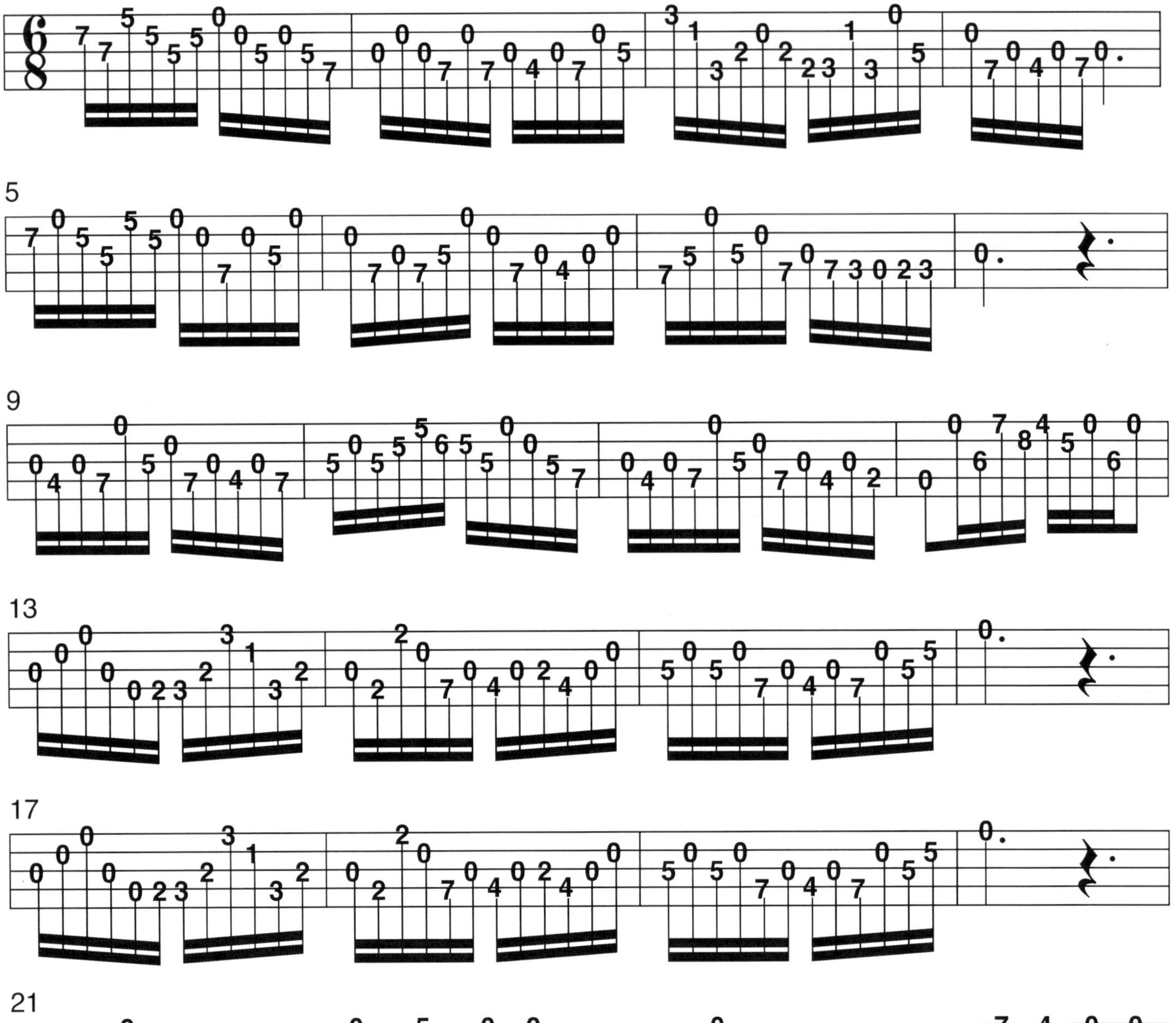

A Lute Lesson (English)

Very often, tunes would come about which were variations or innovations on an instructional exercise. Their source of inspiration was indicated in the title for apparently there was no shame in modeling a tune on such elementary origins. True to the genre, this piece is made up of a number of small phrases, joined together by such things as the same key and the same musical thought. Yet, this example shows that it was forced somewhat into the strophic dance structure as the first 16 measures are very dance-like in character.

It is in A minor, for the most part, yet is one of those Renaissance pieces that resolve themselves to the major in the very last measure. This "lesson" has an unrelated phrase of a few measures added onto the dance structure. This additional phrase, likewise, resolves to the major, in this case A major. Being basically in A minor it uses E major often. G major is seen in the 3rd and 7th measures and in the second measure of the additional phrase. D minor appears in the 9th and 13th measures and in the 3rd measure of the added section.

This version uses the 16th note flurry often, in this instance during A minor runs.

A Lute Lesson

A Major

(English)

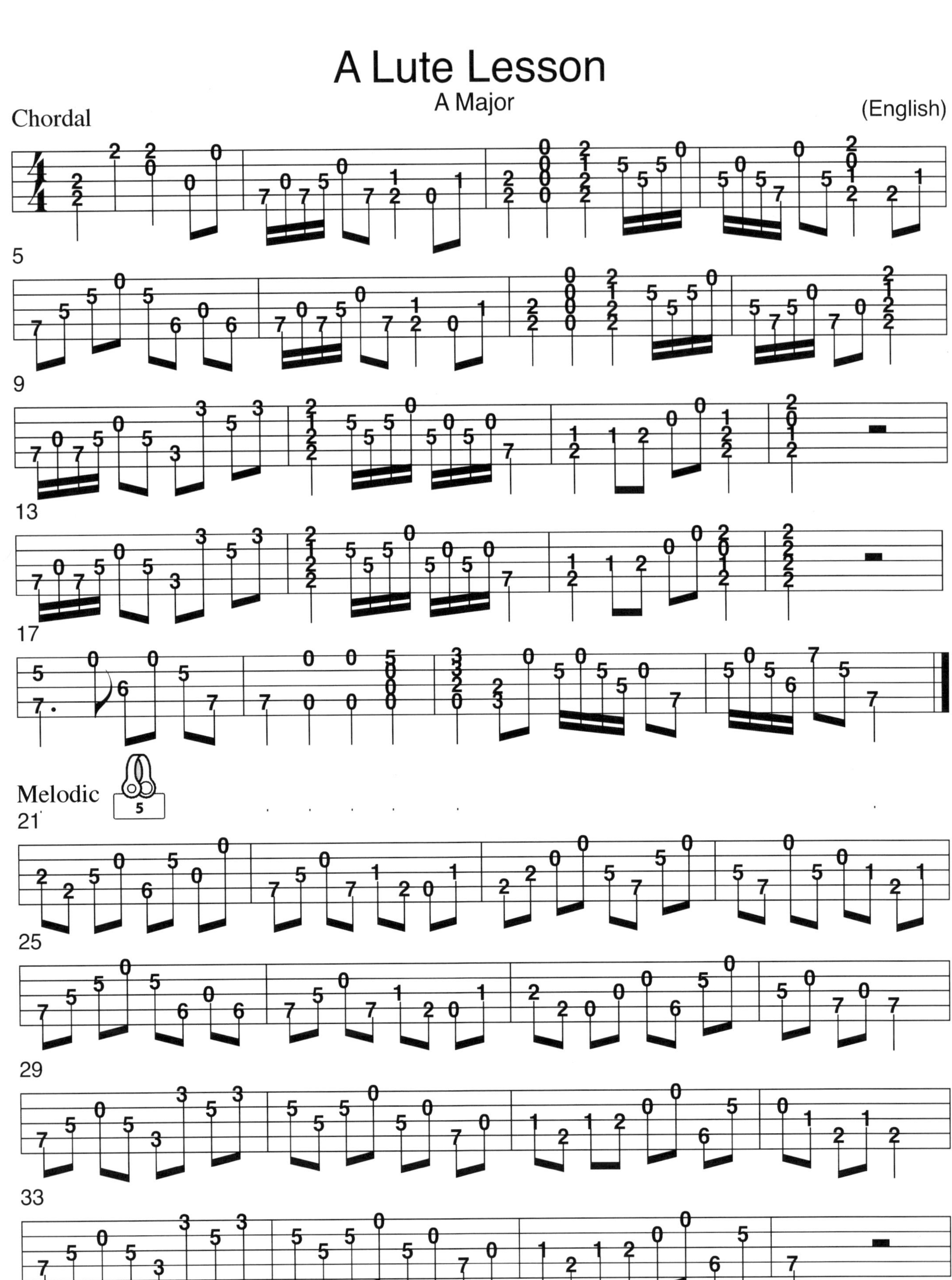

A Pavane (English)

This is an example of a Pavane of the older sort – one that can still be danced to. It is basically structured in the dance form but yet its deviation shows that it was influenced by another form – variations on a theme. The first phrase, measures #1-4 is repeated again in the next phrase measures #5-8, but in a more linear melodic style. Therefore it resembles something somewhere between a dance and a "theme & variations."

The first phrase, measures #1-4 has a march-like plodding feel due to the incessant stream of quarter-note pinches. The musical thought is then repeated in the next phrase but in a smooth fluid melodic style, without the feel of a death march. The first phrase of the second part, measures #9-12 uses a very cautious jumpy hocket. This is actually an ascending scale which is ingeniously interrupted apparently to show apprehension. This apprehension is warranted for the ascending scale which begins in measure #9 in an A note and ends two measures later on an A note, one octave higher. Perhaps A notes are afraid of heights. Measure #12 shows much relief at the successful ascension as it remains in A Major – a comfortable place to be once it has been reached. The last phrase measures #13-16 is simply a lucky fluke. And to prove it, it was ascended again a few measures later in a faster melodic manner. Once more, the success is punctuated with a contented stay in A Major.

The tune is in A Major and remains there for much of the time, using A Major scales to accomplish this. Naturally E Major is used often especially when resolving short phrases as in measures #4 and #8. D Major is encountered and also G Major in the 1st and 5th measures. These two are also used in the ascending scales. B minor is seen in the 3rd, 4th, 7th and 8th measures where it pulls away from and then goes back to E Major.

It is an interesting piece which uses only basic theory yet elaborates on it by the use of variations.

A Pavane

A Major

(English)

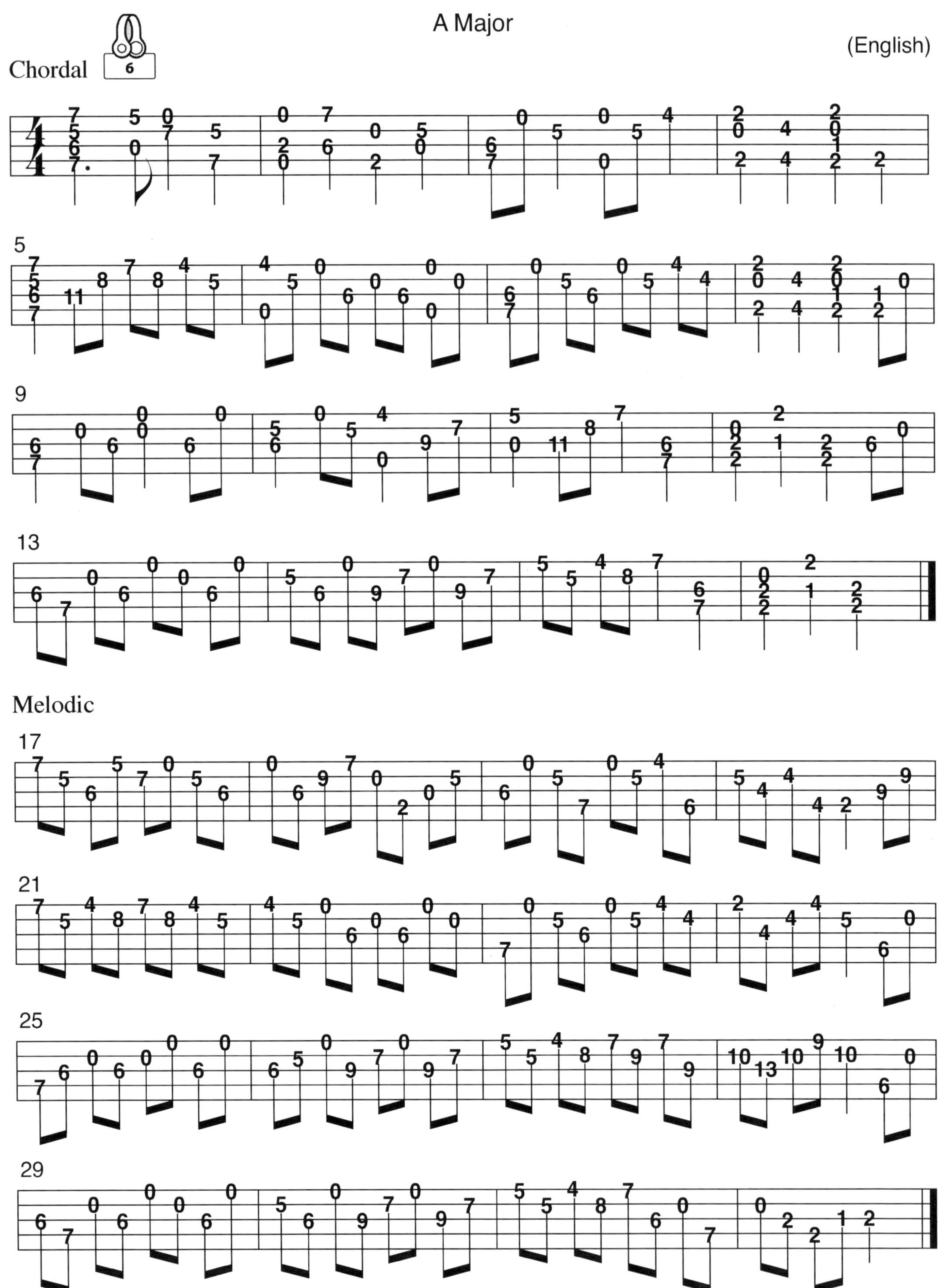

Thomas Robinson (1588-1610): Go From My Window (English)

This is a very simple piece which is a good example of the way in which the Elizabethan mixed art and folk music. The first presentation is done in a very straight forward style which shows the simplistic folk side, while the second is a more complex rendition which can resemble art music. The tune is in D Major and it makes use of A Major and G Major quite often. What makes the piece interesting is the way in which it gravitates between E Major and E Minor in some spots. This was typical of the time period for new tonalities and consonances were being tried and adapted. The B minor chord is used to lead into and pull away from the E Major and E minor passages.

This is a fine example of the "theme and variations" form. Only one musical theme, the first eight measures, is presented. The rest of the work consists of variations of this theme. The piece can be moody. If played very slow it sounds typical of Elizabethan melancholy, but if played briskly it can resemble a fanfare.

The first two measures make a statement in D Major. The next two measures repeat this idea, but in a different key – a good example of imitation. What makes this first phrase interesting is that the responding statement begins in E minor but ends, a measure later in E Major. Besides this peculiarity, the remainder is very straight forward and typical.

Go From My Window

D Major

Thomas Robinson
(English)

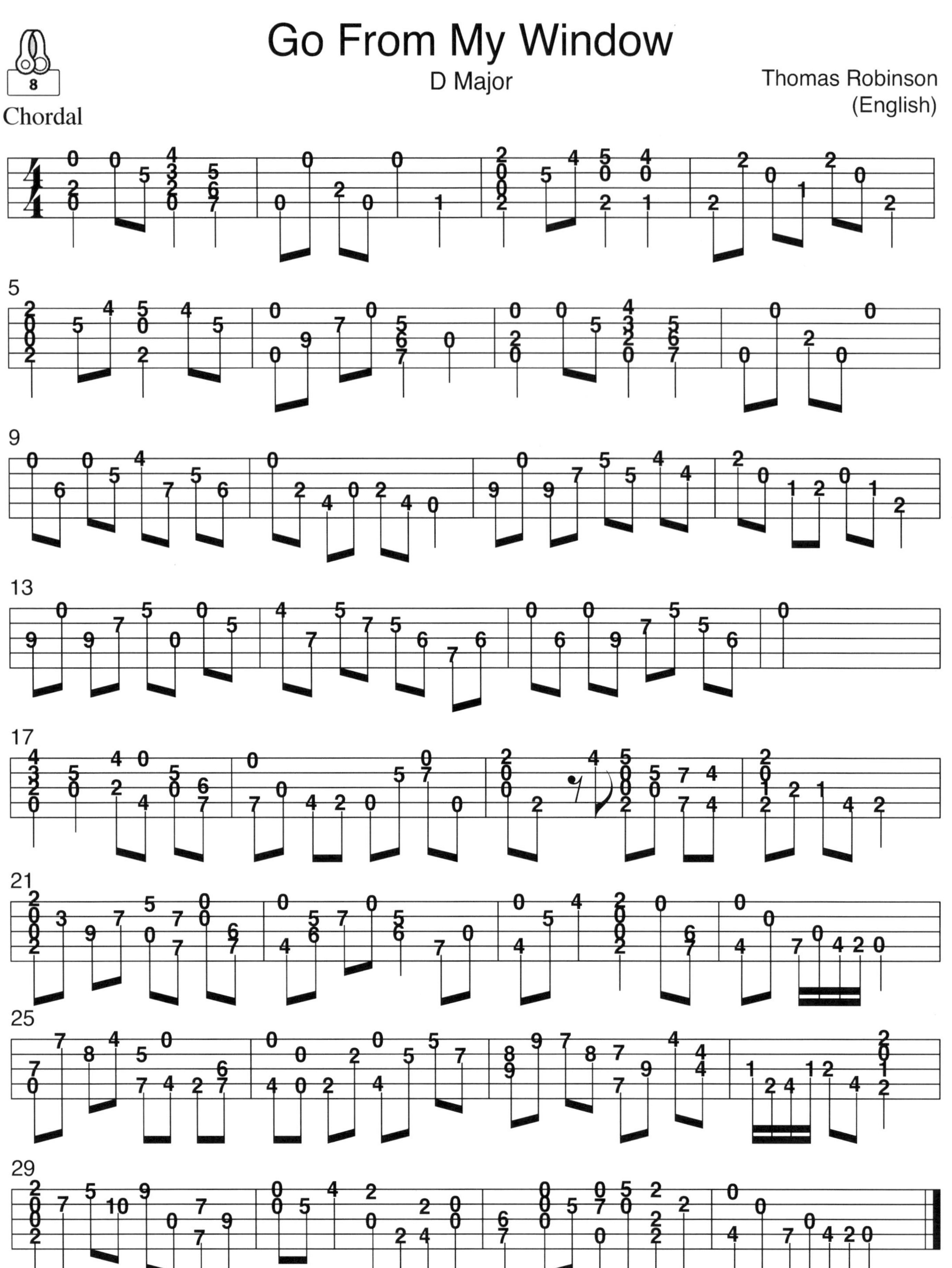

Thomas Robinson (1588-1610): The Queens Jig (English)

This is somewhat difficult due to the fact that harmony plays a big part thus giving it a very "vertical" aspect. This may have been intentional for the chordal relationships are very basic and simple. It also shows another technique for adding spice to a piece of modest theoretical means. The first section is very strophic and dance-like while the second is thorough composed. The second is what gives the tune its flavor.

The first part sounds as if it were a fanfare, and of course this is fitting for after all it was the "Queen's Jig." The second section has a more somber quality. Each measure states a separate musical thought – each distinct yet related. It is almost as if it were a chronological list of all the Queen's noble deeds, each measure representing an act or event. Then a descending run in measures #15-16 seems to act as the crowning glory. Measures #17-21 brings us an incredibly beautiful ending - one which I am so fond of, I adapt it to other pieces as well.

The work is in D Major and so much of the tune revolves around A Major. G Major is entirely lacking and has been replaced by its relative minor, E minor. Chords which are foreign to the key are totally absent. Would the presence of strange chords in the "Queens Jig" be an indication of subversion? Was Robinson covering his tail? The lack of anything foreign or out-of-place is not so surprising once we remember who this was dedicated to. Incidentally, this tune is not theoretically a Jig, for it is in duple 4/4 time, not 6/8. There are a few tunes which exhibit this misnomer, "Kemp's Jig", being perhaps the most well known.

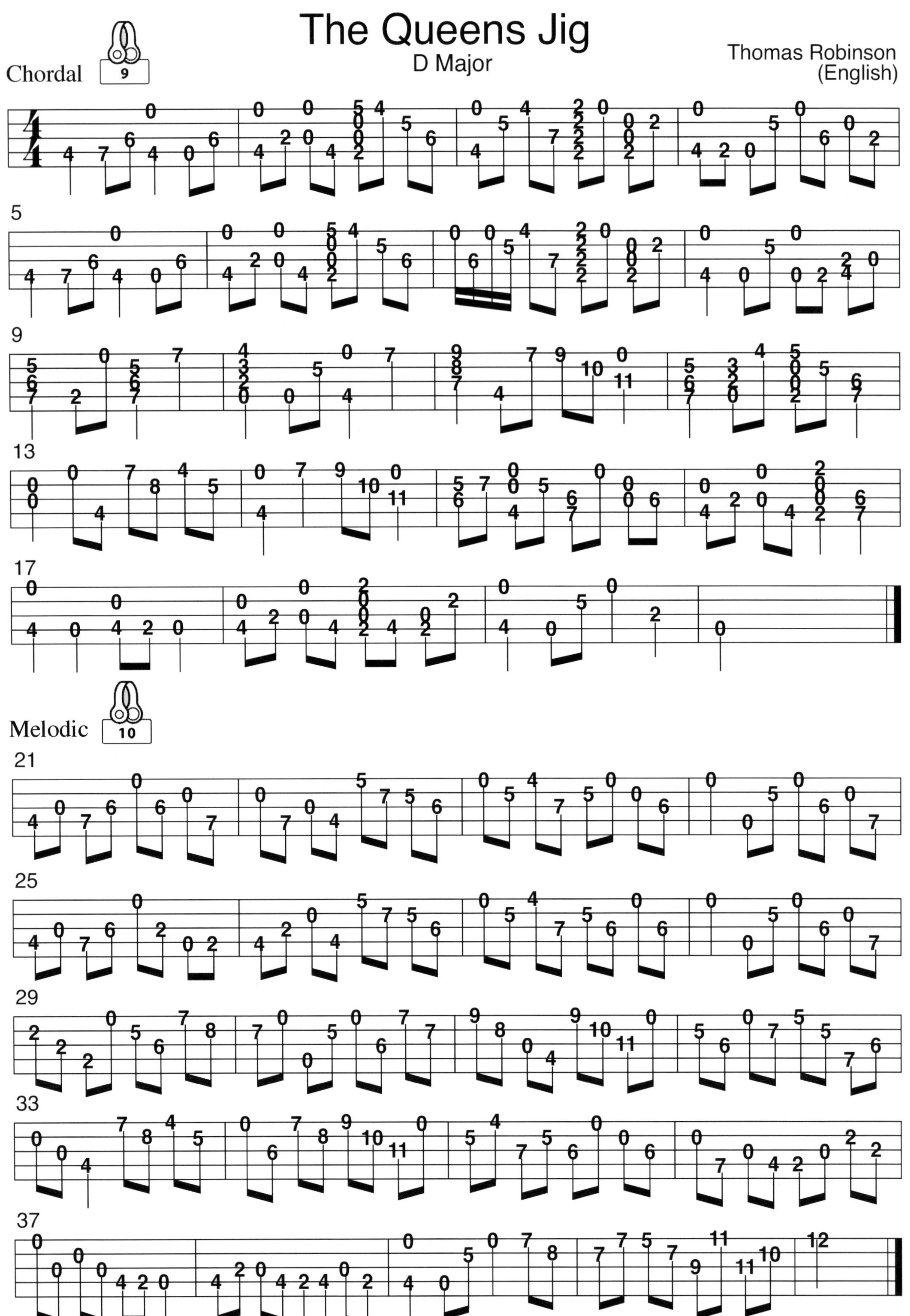
The Queens Jig
D Major
Thomas Robinson
(English)
Chordal
9
Melodic
10

Thomas Campion (1567-1620)
Shall I Come Sweet Love to Thee (English)

I have always had a particular love for this tune. This is probably because it has that haunting eerie sound that can be brought out especially well in the key of D minor. A major is used extensively where its function is to resolve into D minor. B♭ Major makes an appearance in the 2nd measure and then is not to be seen until the end of the tune where he makes his reappearance. F Major, the related major of D minor is used often, along with C Major which is used in its resolutions. A minor makes a two beat debut in the 14th measure only to be never heard from again. In the twelfth measure D Major appears and then vanishes until the very last measure. G minor occurs occasionally while G Major is seen in only one spot – a full chordal strum in the 15th measure.

This is yet another of the many examples that possess that sad, reflective quality which Elizabethan music is famous for. It is thorough-composed consisting of a total of 24 measures. The piece is very pensive throughout yet there are some areas which seem to question this pessimism. It begins with a full strum of a D minor chord in the first measure followed by a single low D note as if to drive home the pessimistic point. A transition from D minor to B♭ Major, F Major and then C Major follows in measure #2. The third measure reinforces the melancholy feel with vertical pinches in G minor which resolves to A Major in the following measure. In measure #5, the doleful feeling gradually evaporates as the mood switches for the better in measures #6, 7 & 8. It is interesting to note how this is accomplished. The phrase begins in D minor, a sad sounding chord, but then resolves into passages using much C Major and F Major – happy sounding chords.

Measures #9 & 10 seem to be questioning the earlier optimism, while the #11 & 12 measures continue the attitude of suspicion. Measures #13-16 indicate that we were on the right track way back in the beginning for much of it is identical to the first four measures. The #17-18 measures continue on in much the same mood, while the vertical pinches in measures #19 & 20 seem to suggest anger. Measures #21 & 22 finally accept the inevitability of the sad situation where the last two measures actually seem to be relieved that this state-of-mind presented itself.

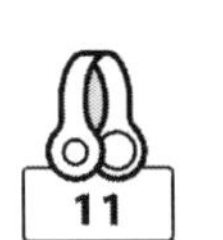

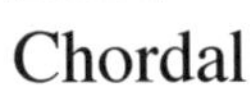

Shall I Come Sweet Love to Thee

D Minor

Chordal

Thomas Campion
(English)

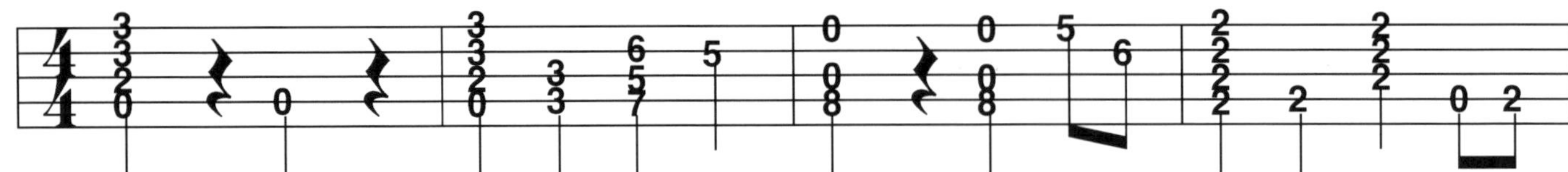

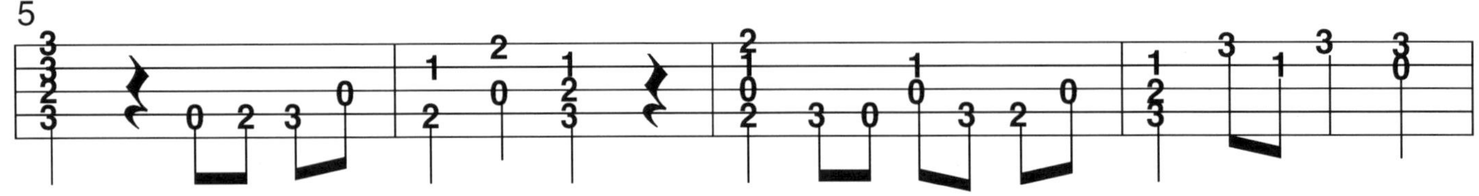

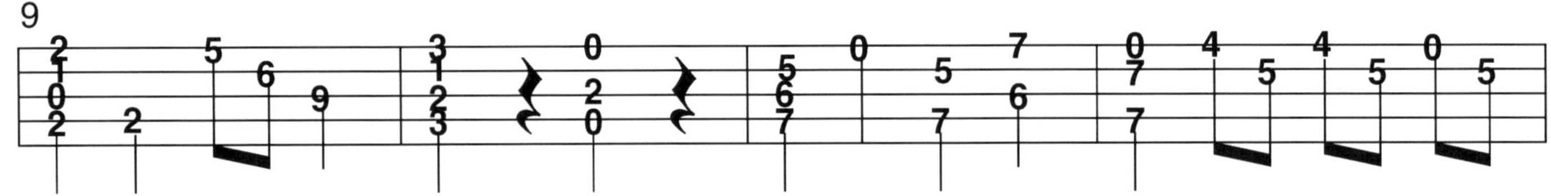

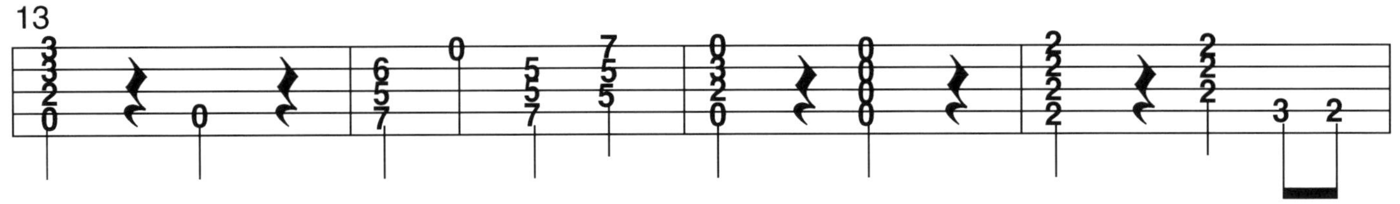

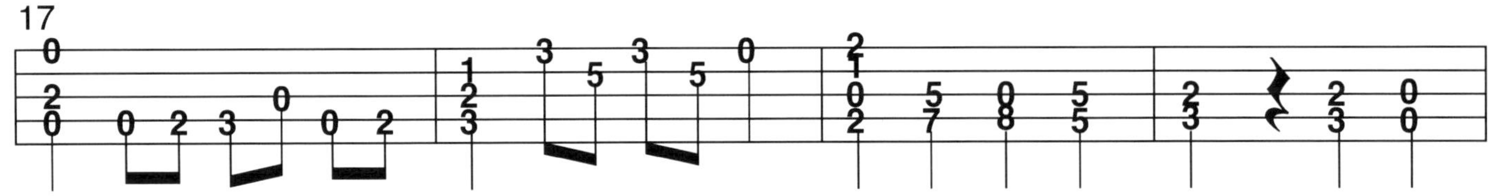

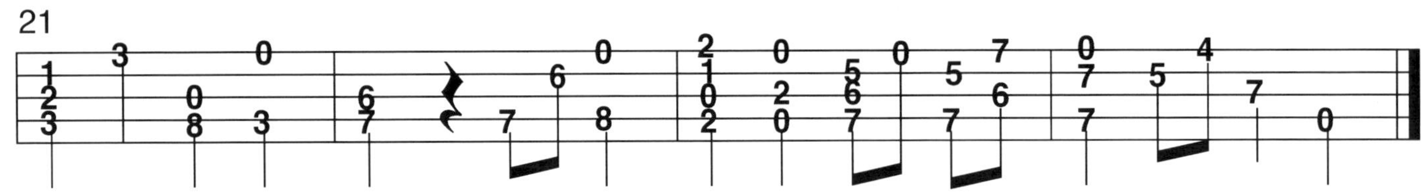

Shall I Come Sweet Love to Thee

D Minor

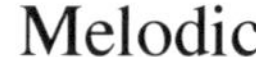

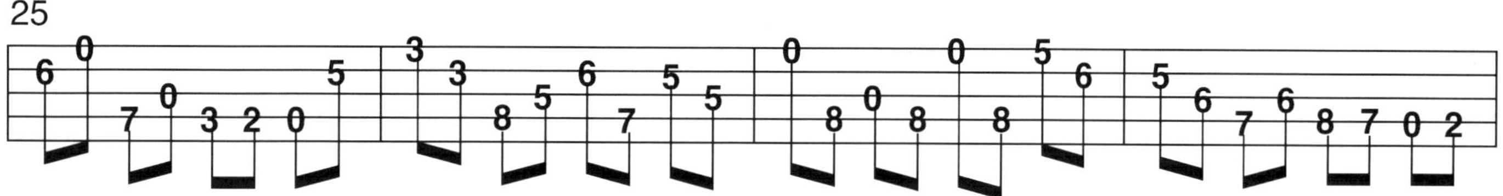

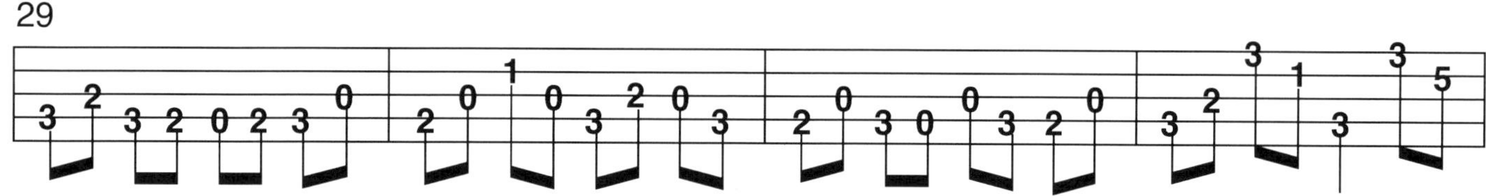

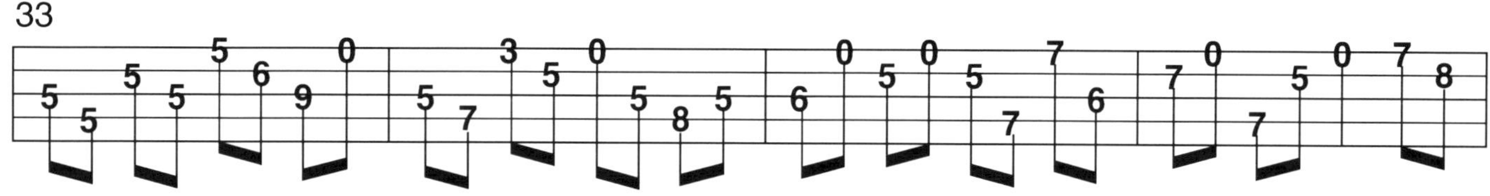

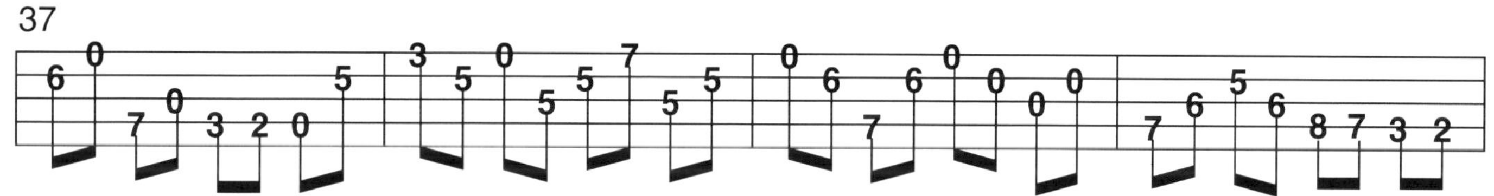

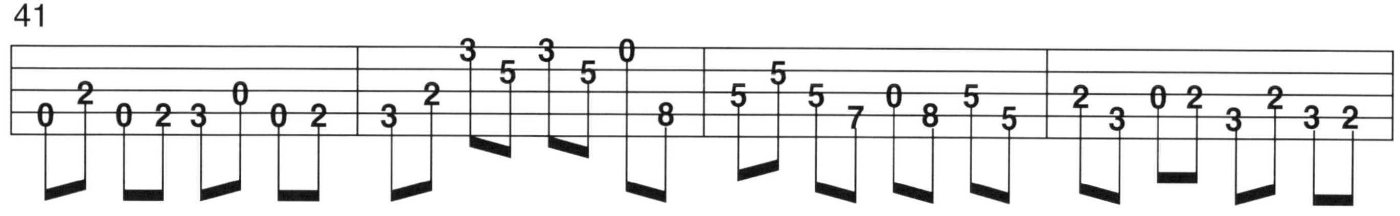

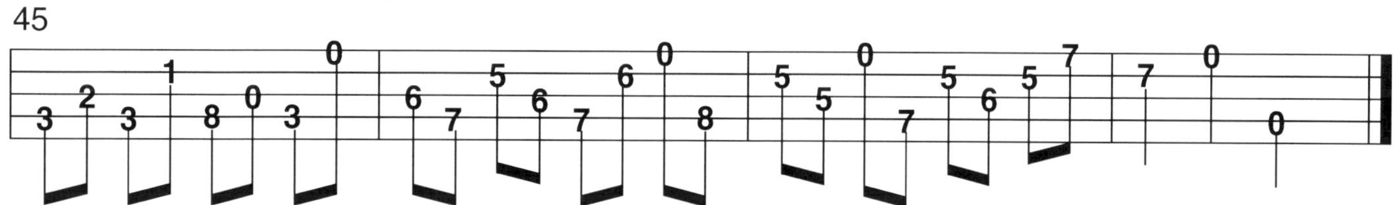

Thomas Campion (1567-1620)
Never Weather Beaten Sail (English)

This tune resembles "Shall I Come Sweet Love to Thee" in some ways, but it is in the key of F Major, which is the relative major of D minor, the key that the other piece is in. It uses C Major and B♭ Major much to the exclusion of all other chords, which makes this a relatively unsophisticated tune. Yet, the concept of harmony is applied well here. It shows that a good composer can take only three chords and weave a work of art using the individual "threads" of those chords. It also exhibits an interesting Renaissance cadence which utilizes the F Major (added 4th) chord. The tune is typical of those that express the Elizabethan man's state of depression – real or imagined. It practically cries out at you to slow down and respect its solemn intricacies. You are warned of this early on for after the first beat a full quarter rest is thrown at you as a roadblock. And after that, a number of quarter note pinches. When a flurry of 8th notes is finally encountered in the 3rd measure, you are encouraged to speed up but only long enough for a resolution to F Major in the following four measures. Measure #13 brings in a new feeling, an alternative to what the preceding musical message was leading to. It almost sounds as if it had a new idea, but then rejected it only three measures later. By the 17th measure it feels as if the entire musical thought had been abruptly curtailed, and thus wanting to forget the whole matter, a good ending was immediately tacked on. The fact that the piece uses 18 measures – a rather odd number also suggests that the musical thought met a premature demise. Could we say that this shows the nihilism of the times?

Never Weather Beaten Sail

F Major

Thomas Campion
(English)

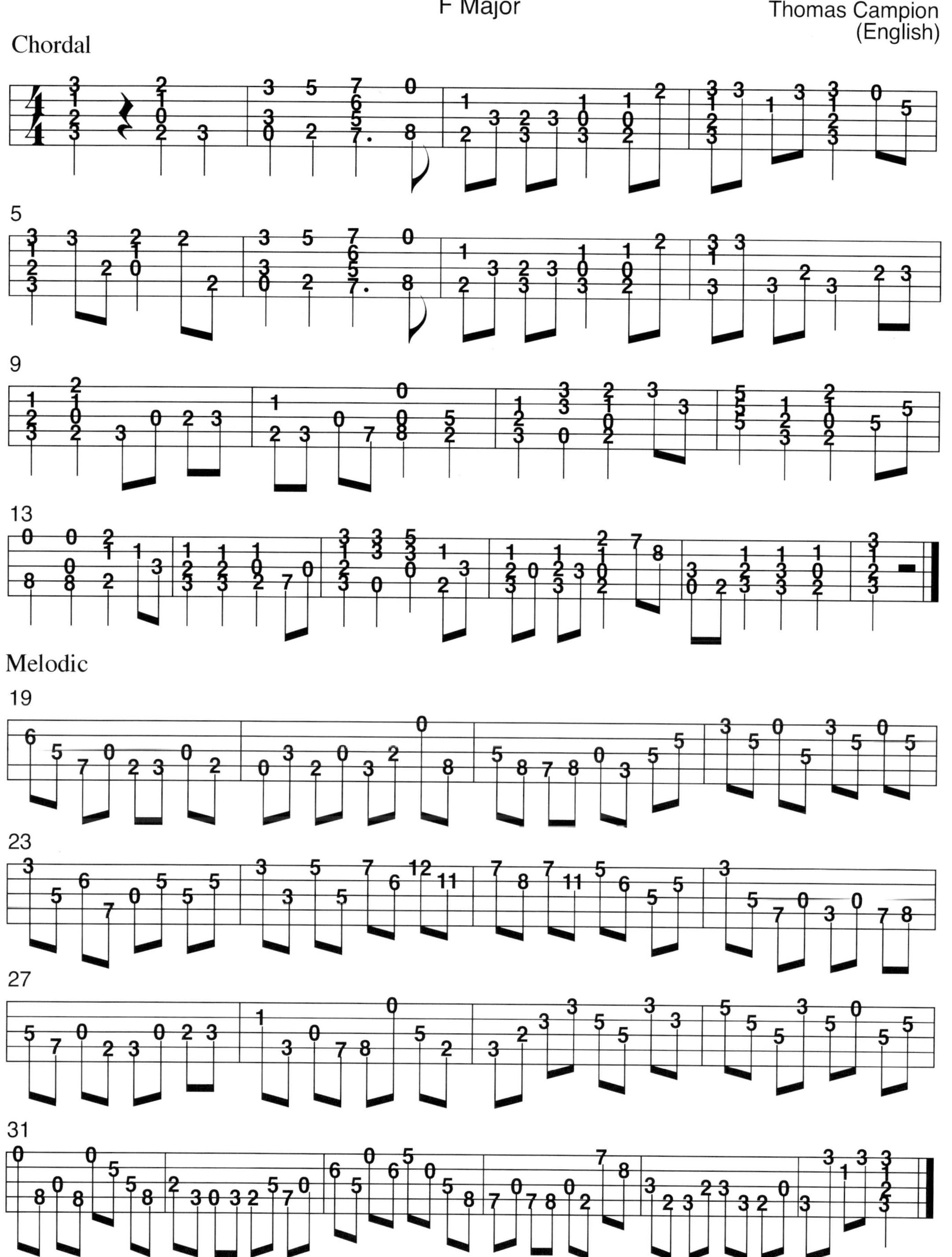

John Dowland (1563-1626)
Come Again (English)

This is a wonderous piece by the all-time master. It is totally thorough-composed with no traits of the dance. It begins in the mood we have come to expect of Dowland, melancholy, but gradually works away from this until an excited state cannot be denied. The first four measures are typical of Dowland depression, yet in measures #5 & 6 he seems to be reconsidering his somber state. Apparently, he convinced himself that he had been wrong all along and an exhilarating ascending run which lasts for the next three measures is the result. But even this he reconsiders in measures #10-12. Again he tries to be optimistic for the following three measures as he repeats the ascending run once more. This time the phony euphoria is embellished by 16th-note flurries as if it would be of some help. This is apparently unsuccessful for the entire idea, measures #7-17, is repeated in full and then finally capped off with a typical, but no less beautiful Renaissance ending.

The work is in D Major, and so A Major is common. G Major has been replaced in most places by its relative minor, E minor. It only survives in the euphoric ascensions in the 9th and 15th measures. E Major is used in the 6th measure simply to resolve to A Major. A7 shows up in the second measure where it resolves to D Major. This was a very common technique of the times and was used to great advantage by Elizabethan composers. F♯ minor is seen in the 8th measure where it is part of that ascending run. The run begins in D Major, then E minor, to G Major, A Major and then resolves back to D Major again. B minor is seen, for a very brief spell in the 11th measure to resolve into an E minor in the 12th.

One of my favorites, due to the twists, turns and that fantastic ascending run

Come Again

D Major

John Dowland
(English)

Chordal

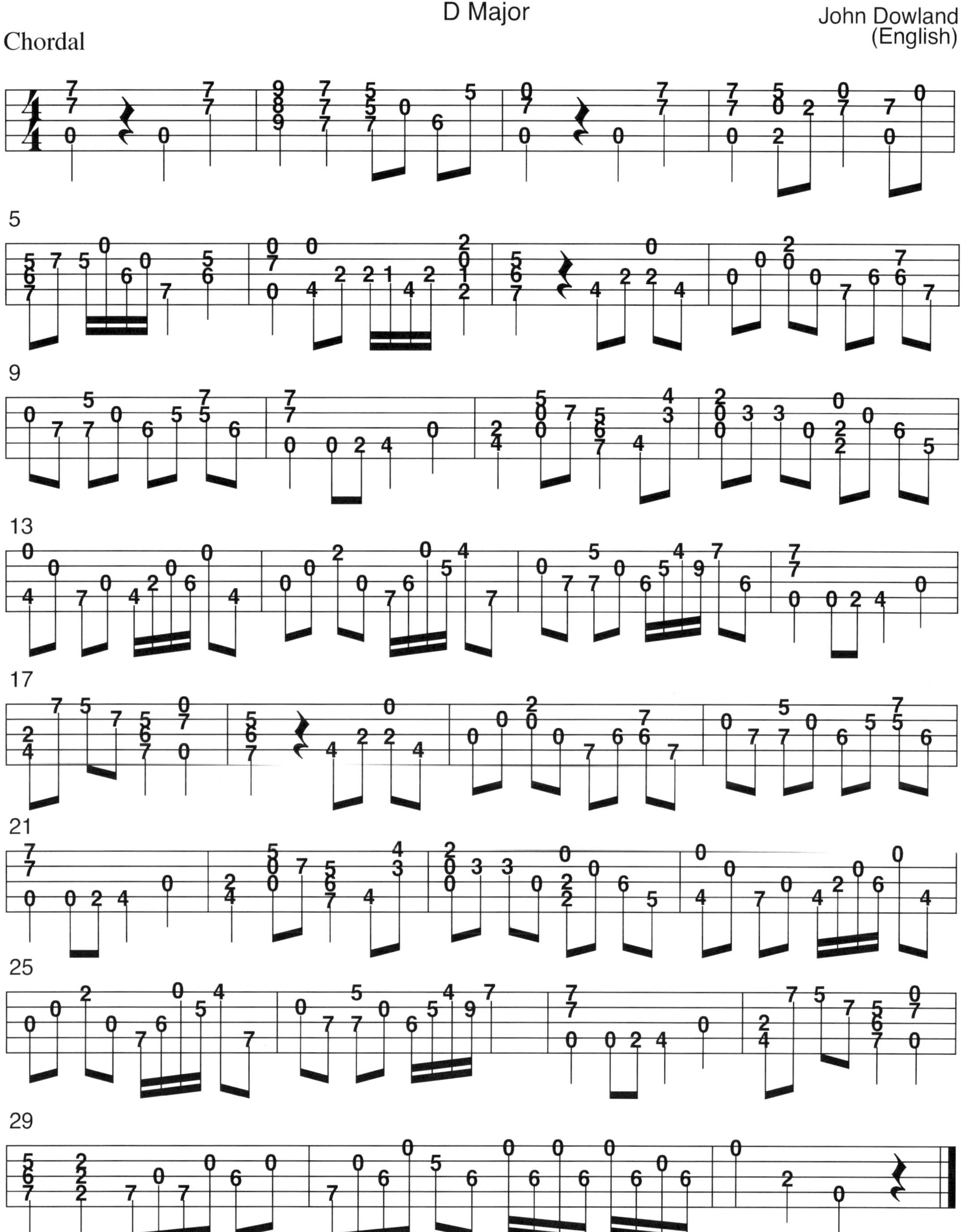

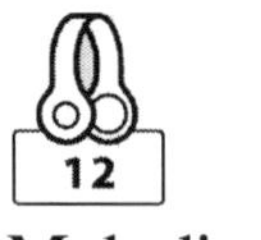

Melodic

Come Again

D Major

John Dowland
(English)

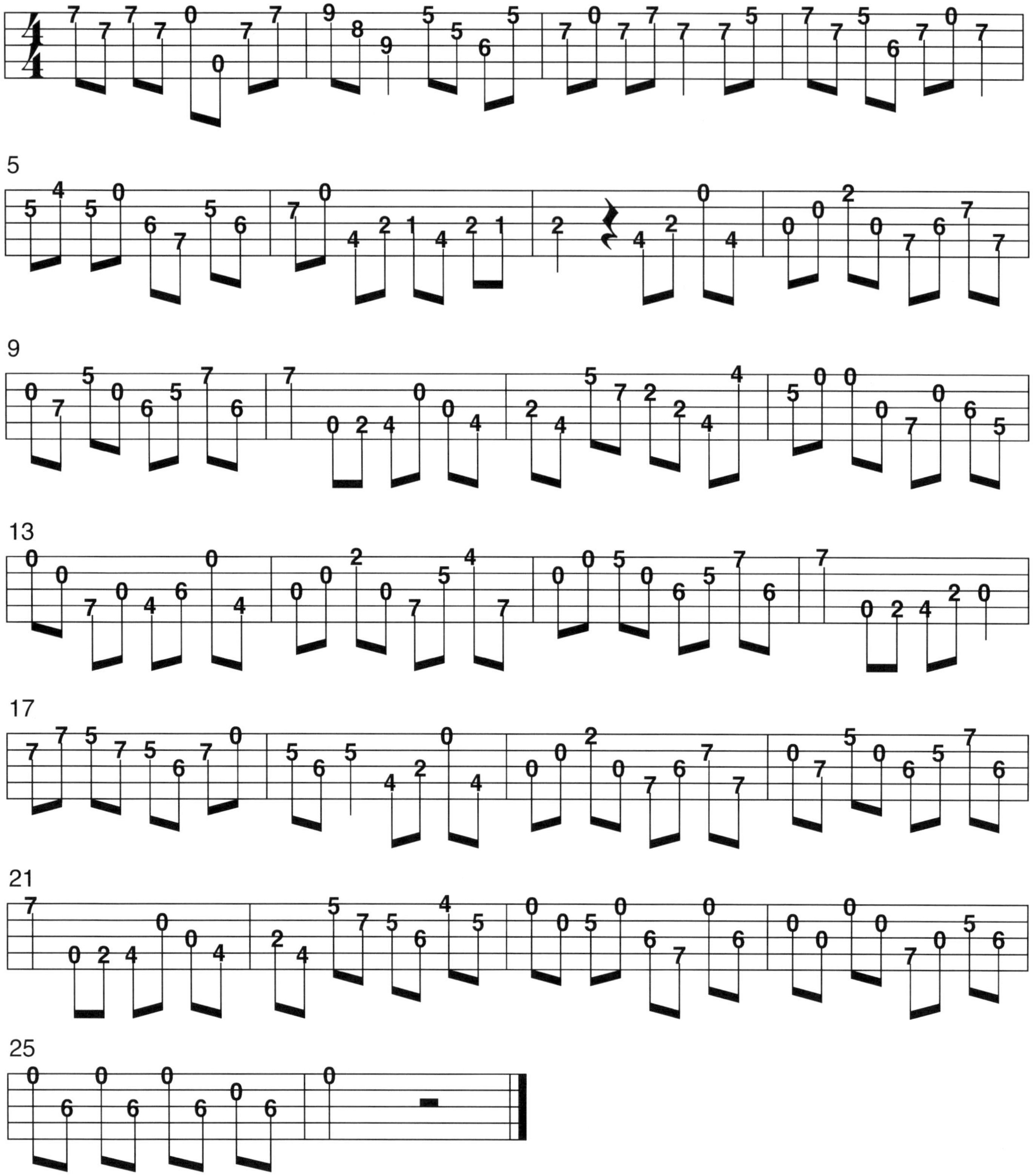

John Dowland (1563-1626)
Lachrimae Pavane (English)

This one may prove to be a bit tough, but it is well worth the effort. It is presented here as an instrumental, labeled a pavane, but in its day it was sometimes given a text and treated as an ayre. It was then known as "Flow My Tears." As a pavane it falls naturally into dance form of two sections of eight measures each. Since Dowland would be Dowland it has that melancholy feel throughout.

Typical of the times it begins in a minor key and ends in its major, here going from A minor to A Major. There are many twists and turns which keep it fresh and interesting. It starts out rather doleful, tries to free itself from this in the third measure, but then descends back down in the fourth. It remains there for the duration of the following phrase, measures #5-8.

The second section begins with its head held high, but again falls on hard times in the 11th measure. It tries to pick itself up again in measure #12 but this is apparently ineffective for what follows is the most depressing passage of the entire tune and then the ending. One gets the feeling that the 16th-note flurries scattered throughout are used to express frustration. Frustration at not being able to pull out of this depressive state. This is especially true of the 12th measure where a double flurry is followed by an optimistic high A note.

Most of the piece is in A minor. It only transforms to A Major at the end of each section. It should not be surprising to find E Major in proliferation, often being replaced with E minor. C Major, the relative major of A minor is found in the 3rd and 6th measures while F Major is encountered in the 4th, 7th & 9th measures. Both G Major and B Major are found in only one spot, the 9th and 13th measures respectively. A very unusual chord, F Major 7, is used in the 2nd and 6th measures to express reflection. The end of the 16th century and the beginning of the 17th was a time when new chords and harmonies, such as this one were being experimented with.

This is a very rich piece. One where every measure or short phrase has its own musical thought. So much is contained within each individual measure. Special techniques are used to much advantage. Measures #9-10 uses vertical block strums to express a noble, unflinching character. The Renaissance device of taking a full chord and sliding it back a half tone is employed, here going from F Major to E Major. The fourth measure shows a nice descending run, while measure #13 has low notes dueling with the higher in the B Major chord.

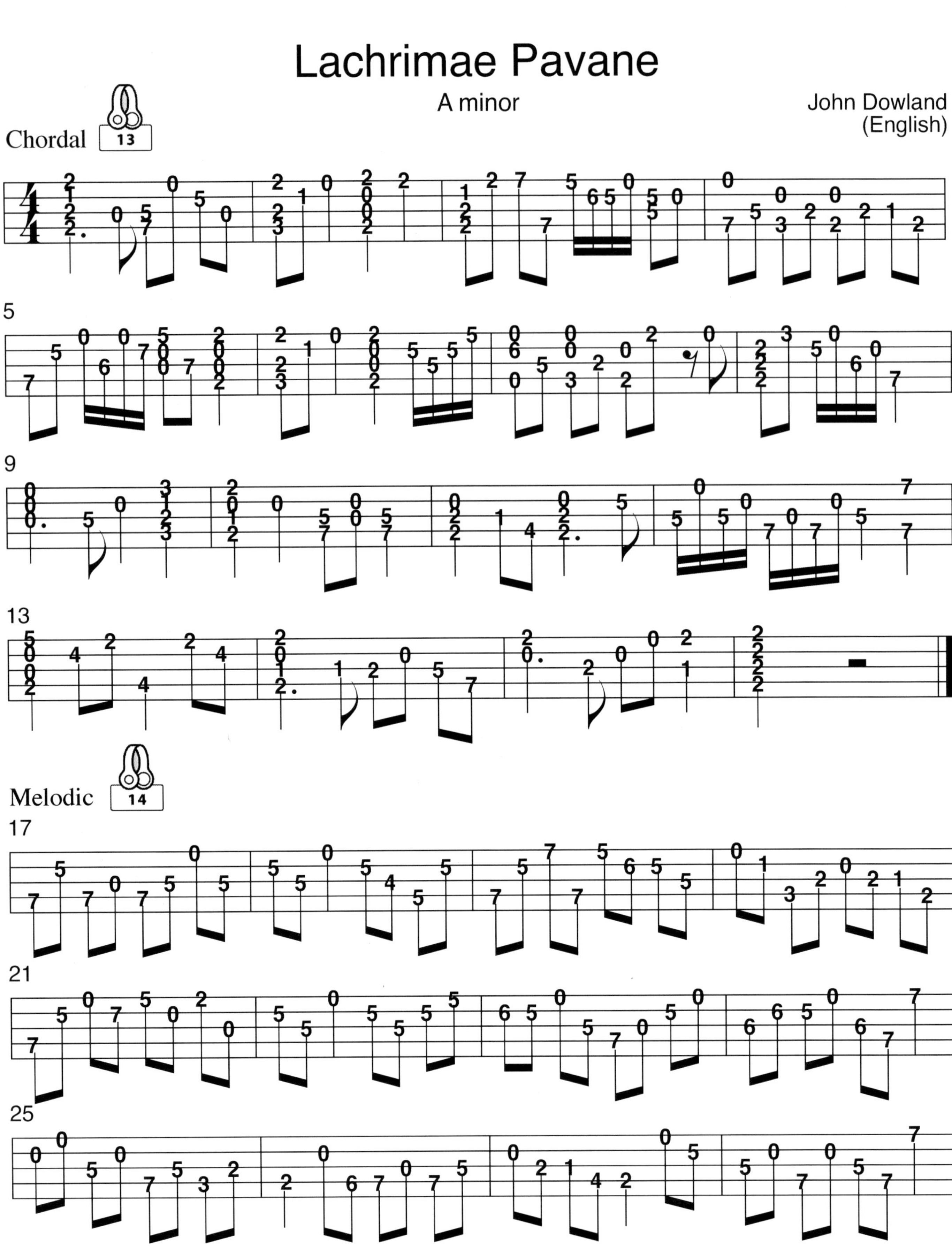
Lachrimae Pavane
A minor
John Dowland
(English)
Chordal
13
Melodic
14

John Dowland (1563-1626)
A Pavane (English)

Didn't Dowland ever write happy tunes? Apparently not!! This is another plodding pensive pavane. It appears to be in dance form but upon closer scrutiny one can see that it is somewhat thorough-composed. It probably originated as a dance but had gradually become stylized.

It begins on a rather happy note yet the A minor chord in the second measure is a hint at what is yet to come. The mood gets very sour by the end of the fourth measure with the B minor chord. It remains that way for the next phrase – measures #5-8. To really rub in the pessimistic atmosphere the performers that I have heard would play the flurries in measures #17-19 gradually slower when it approached the end. This helps set the mood. A musical thought is presented in measures #9-11 which is then slightly varied in the next three measures. It then bursts into a frenzy of flurries which last until the end of the piece. This extreme excitement, which goes on for seven entire measures appears to be wanting to back away from the rest of the piece. This is all in vain for by the last measure, the flurries again gradually slow down as he runs out of gas during his escape.

The work is in D Major throughout. G Major is found quite often in the first section while in the second it is absent. Just the opposite is true for A Major. B minor is found in measures #4, 5 & 11. A minor is seen in measures #2 and 5, while C Major is found only in measure #9. This piece also has rare appearances by some unusual chords. The 5th measure contains a F♯ minor, while the 15th has an A7. A Major (with an added 2nd), a chord somewhat common in Renaissance music, shows up here in measures #10 & 12, where it acts as a catalyst.

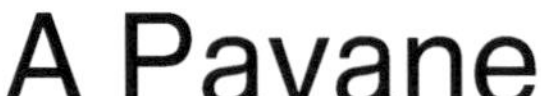

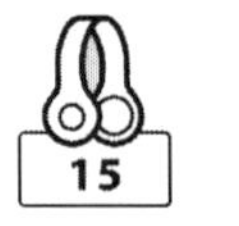

D Major

John Dowland
(English)

Chordal

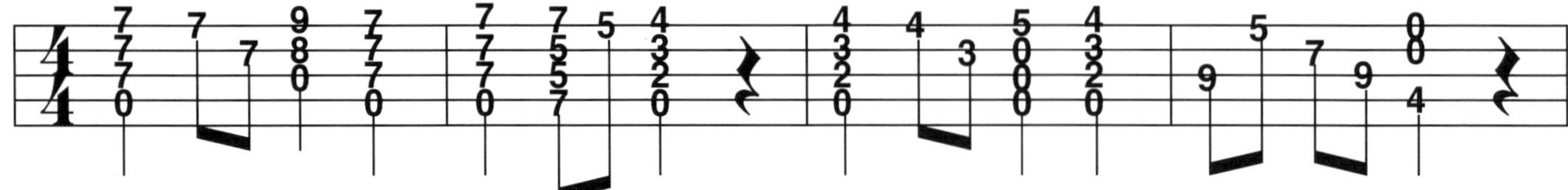

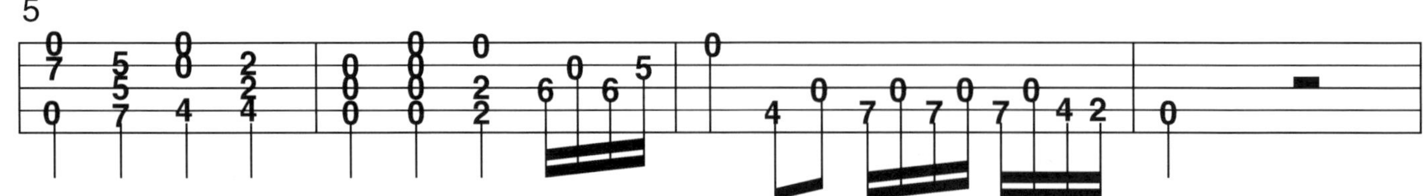

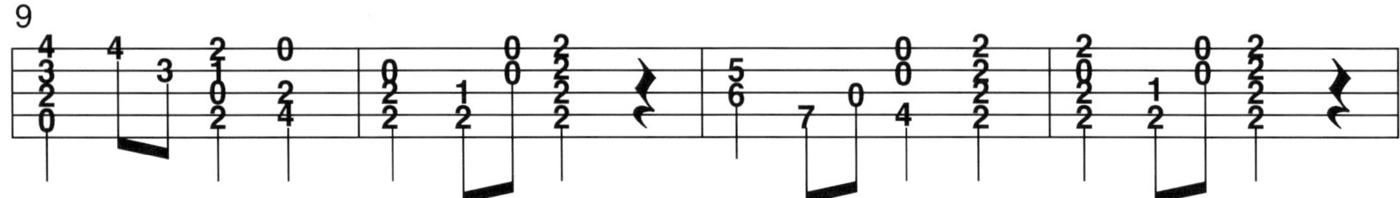

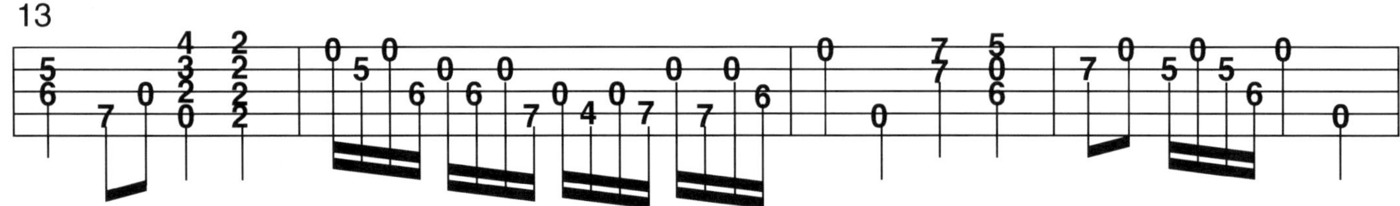

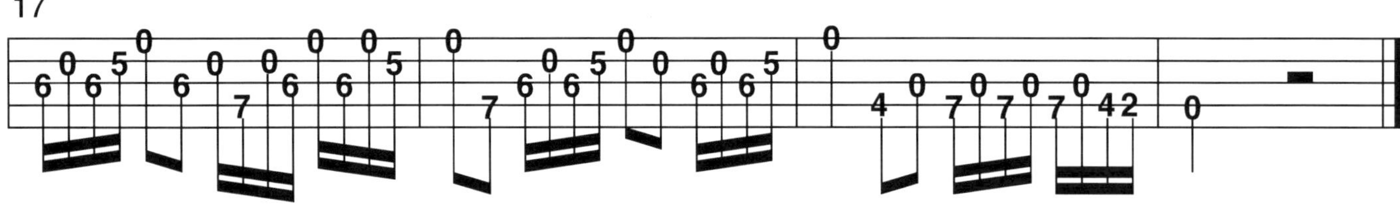

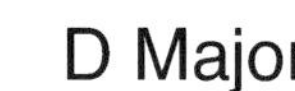

A Pavane

D Major

John Dowland
(English)

16

Melodic

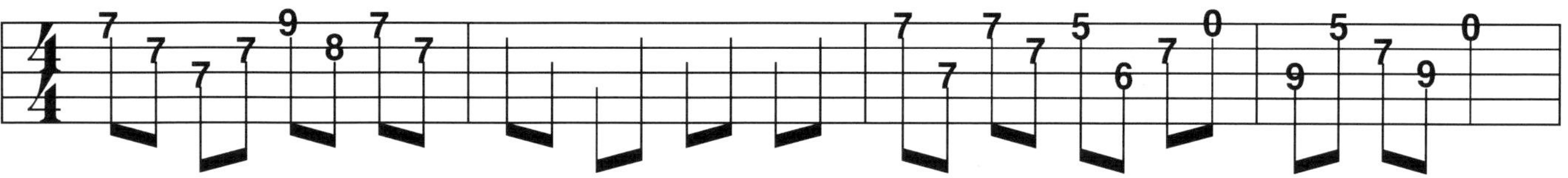

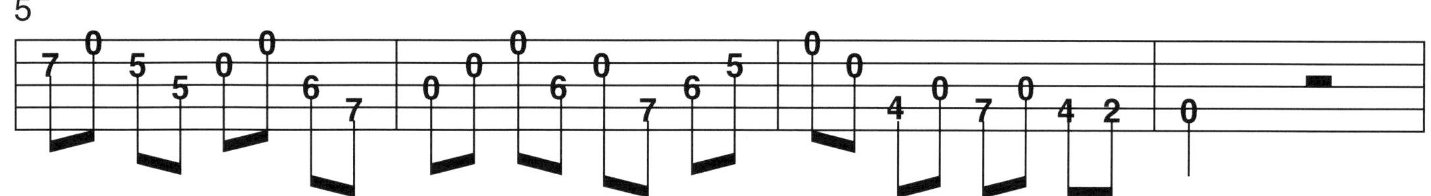

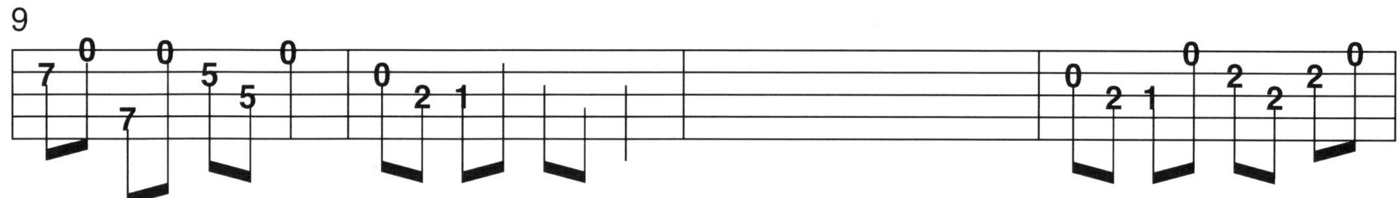

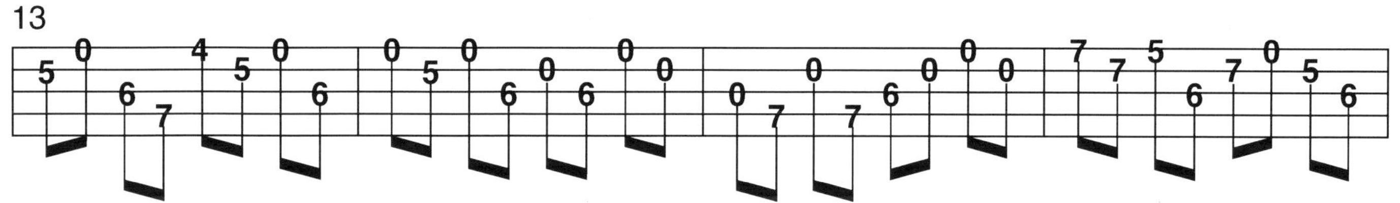

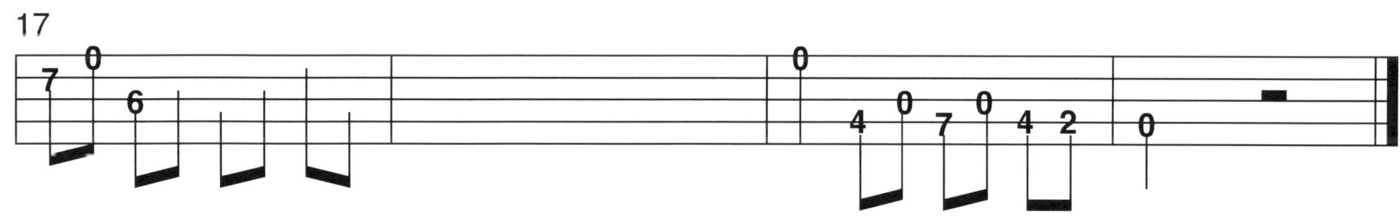

John Dowland (1563-1626)
A Ballet (English)

The joyful nature of this piece causes one to suspect that Dowland was not the real author. All joking aside, he actually did write some upbeat material although he is not known for it. This is one example. It is in typical dance form but with the second section lengthened to ten measures instead of the usual eight. There is really nothing too outstanding about it yet it does have a couple of interesting quirks. The bass run in measures #9-10 and #13-15 give it a refreshing quality. This is especially true where flurries are interspersed within. 16th-note flurries are quite common in the second part, while they are entirely lacking in the first. The proliferation of them in the latter half gives the impression that the performer has mastered the piece and gained confidence – enough to engage in a bit of showing off. The ending of the first section, measures #7-8 has a very strong concrete feel to it. This is then continued for measures #9-10, breaks away from it in the next few measures and then returns in the 13th measure. It then breaks away again in a cluster of flurries and ends in a high-register passage.

The piece is in D Major and so A Major is common. G Major is conspicuous by its absence being replaced by its relative minor – E minor. E Major is seen quite often, usually being used to resolve into A Major. B minor makes a rare appearance in the third measure, while A7 is seen only in the second.

A Ballet

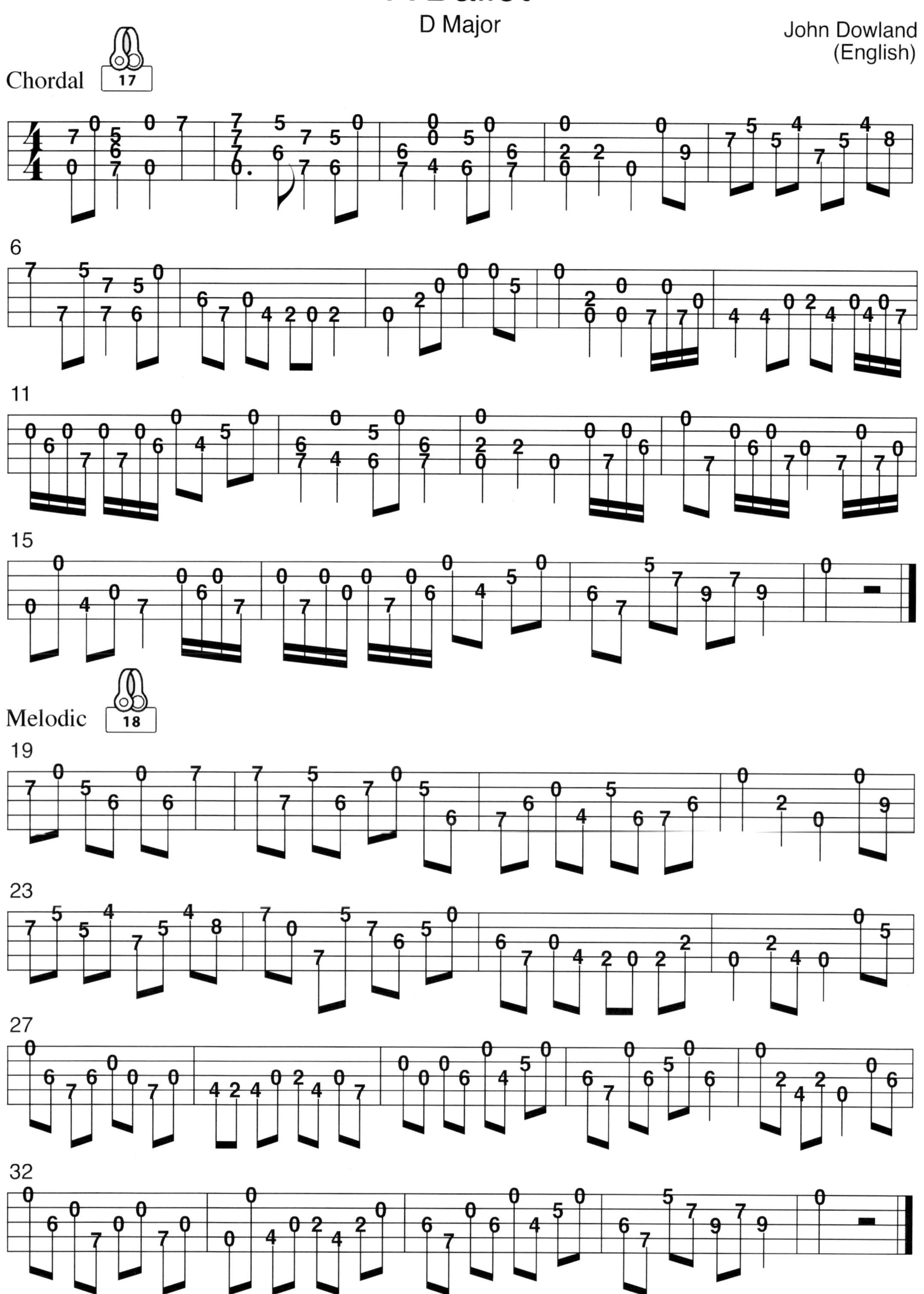

This page has been left blank to avoid awkward page turns.

John Dowland (1563-1626)
Melancholy Galliarde (English)

One of my all-time favorites – Dowland at his best. When playing at Renaissance Fairs I like to explain to the patrons that it was fashionable to be depressed during the 16th century and then proceed to prove it by breaking into this tune. It is a stylized dance which exhibits some interesting twists.

As the name suggests, this tune is to be played slow. Depression is expressed yet there is often the feeling that the composer is trying to break away from it. This can be seen in the first measure alone. It begins in a sad-sounding D minor chord which in the same measure transforms itself into the happy-sounding D Major. The next two measures lead us to believe that this was only a farce and Dowland lapses back into depression with a low F Major in the fourth measure. But ever so resilient he bounces back again by ascending to a high D minor in measure #5 and keeps his chin up for the remainder of the section.

But this he cannot keep up for long as he becomes pensive in measures #9-12 where he ponders his condition. Again in measures #13-16 he tries to be optimistic but then falls back into that low F Major chord. He then begins to air his ultimate complaint beginning in the 17th measure. The intensity of his anguish is felt in the way it is presented using harsh quarter-note strums while descending to the low A Major in measure #20. Dowland has already hit bottom for in the last four measures he laments his fate. Even though the piece ends in a major chord, there is no hint of optimism at all. Perhaps this is the irony of the tune. Dowland and his ilk are in such a state that not even a major chord ending can cure. They even take the upbeat Galliarde and turn it sour.

This is another one of these tunes that begin in a minor chord and end in its major. The piece is predominately in D minor, yet it is sometimes substituted with a D Major such as in measures #2 and 8. Chords closely related to D minor, such as A Major, G Major, C Major and F Major are all present. B♭ Major is encountered usually associated with F Major as in measures #5, 14, 15, 19, 21 and 22. A rare encounter with G minor occurs in the 19th measure where it resolves in A Major. C7 is seen in the 21st and 22nd measures where it acts as a catalyst between F Major and B♭ Major. The single string staccatos in thc 9th and 13th measures add a refreshing touch.

Melancholy Galliarde

19

Chordal

D minor

John Dowland
(English)

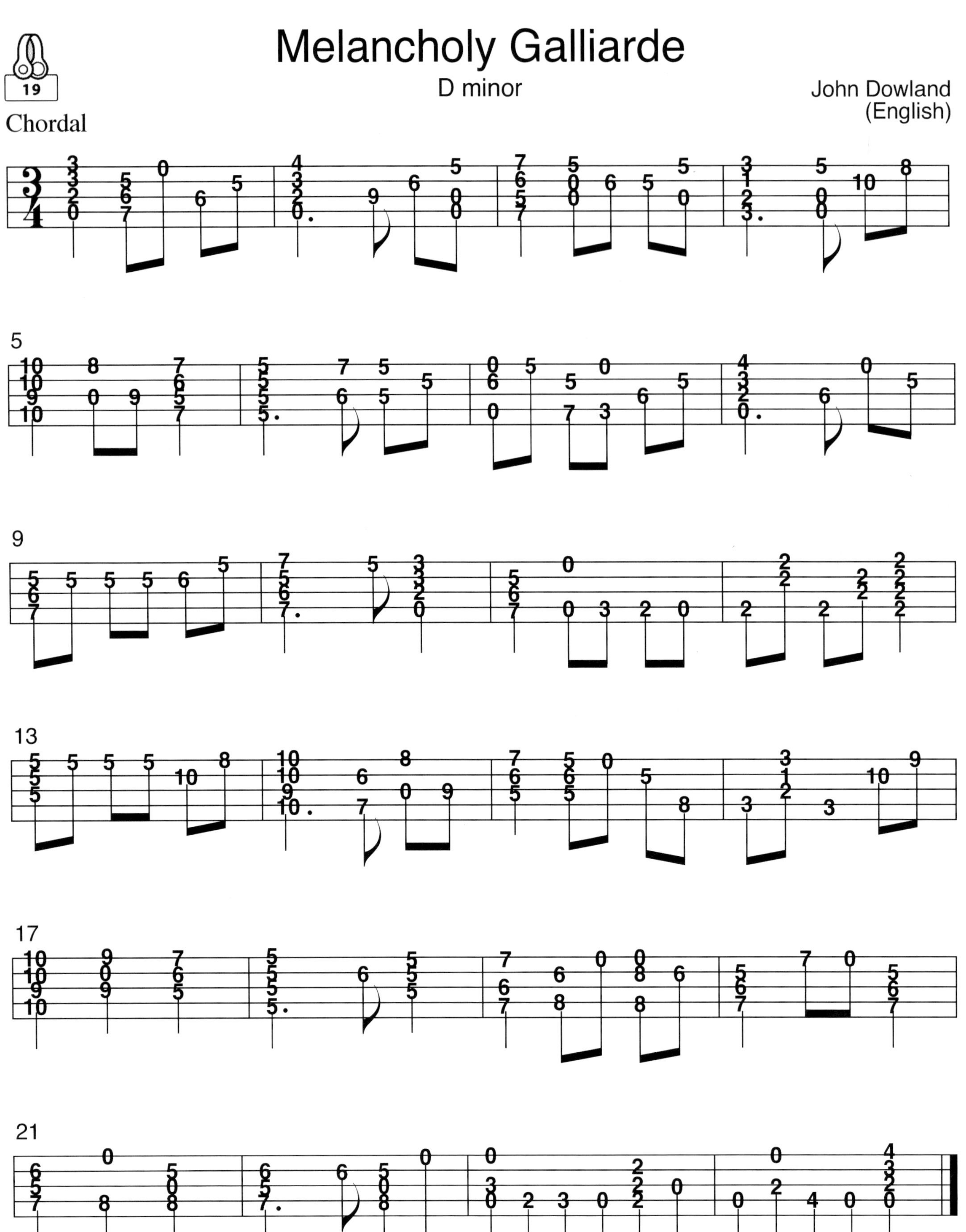

Melancholy Galliarde

D minor

John Dowland
(English)

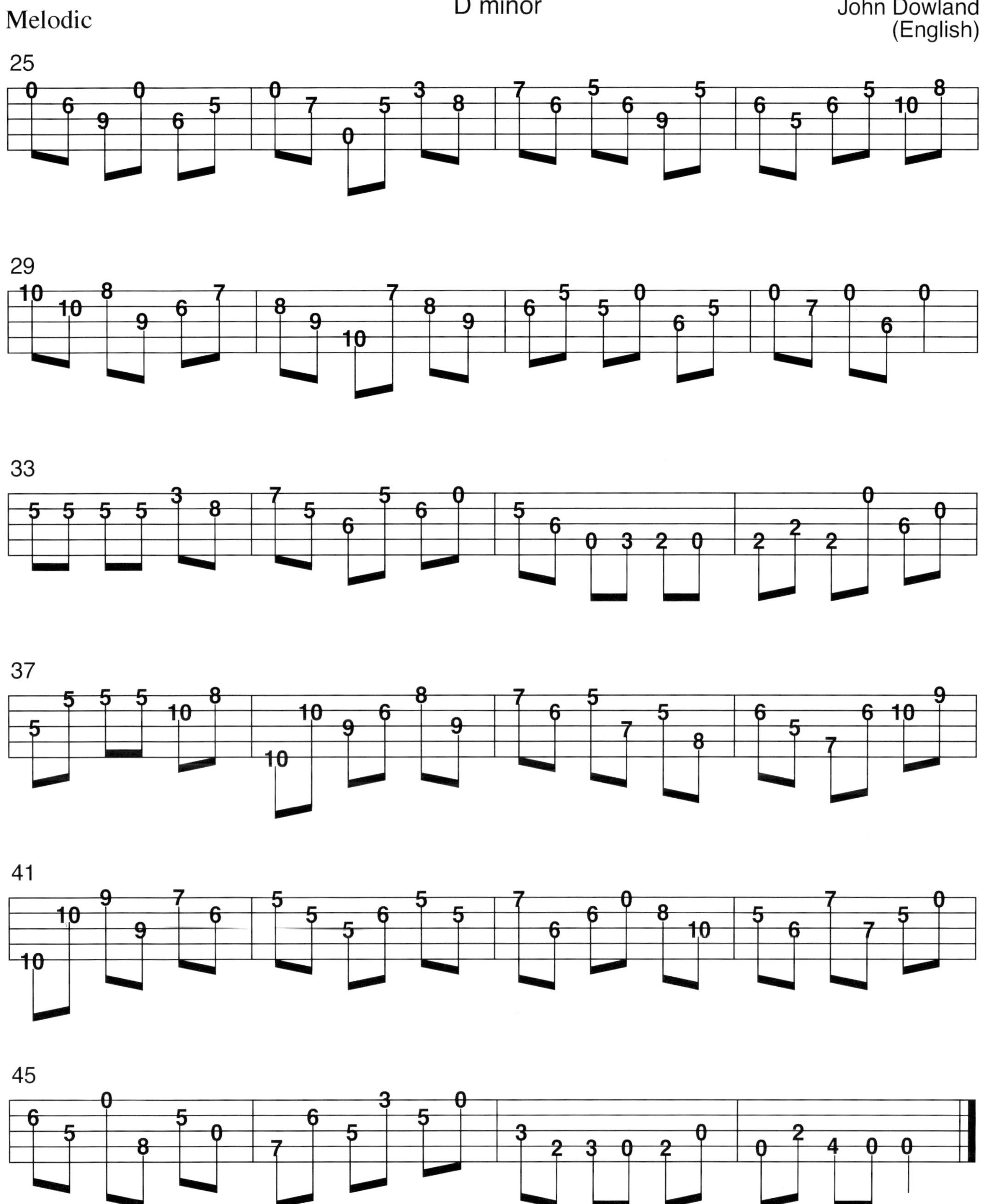

Anthony Holborne (1547-1602)
A Galliarde (English)

In my opinion this is one of the most beautiful pieces ever written. I first heard it from a recording called “Tabernakel” by Jan Akkerman. It contains the most inspiring music that I have ever been exposed to and I have been affected by it considerably. He plays Archlute, which gives an extremely rich, full sound in the bass register. Akkerman’s treble is truly ethereal and floats heavenward while his bass seems as if it can penetrate the deepest watery depths. His Archlute playing must be heard to be appreciated. Sadly, I believe that it is out of print.

When people ask me to name my favorite piece I often reply, “A Galliarde,” by Anthony Holborne.” Puzzled, they inquire “A Galliarde, he wrote a number of them, which one??” This illustrates a big problem when discussing music of the period. Sometimes a musician may compose a dance for a patron, and then name it after them. Other times a tune would be composed and given a very generic title such as “a dance” or perhaps no title at all. This gets to be incredibly annoying to the modern musicologist who loves to taxonomize and pigeon-hole everything in neat packaged categories. They also come to despise it when people ask them their favorite tune. I assume that it was the fashion at the time to give pieces non-descript generic titles; for little mental exertion is called for to think of a catchy title and I have never met a musician who does not relish this.

This wonderful piece is a good example of a stylized dance which has evolved to be practically thorough-composed. It is also another piece which when played slow is pensive but when played briskly sounds like a fanfare. It is interesting for it can be moody even though it is in a major key. When played as a fanfare it sounds very stately but when played calmly the character of the piece comes out. This is how Akkerman treated it, and so that is how we shall look at it here.

The beginning is somewhat startling for the first three notes ascend very rapidly. This may catch some off guard as the beginning of a tune usually is not this animated. It goes from a low D to a high D within the space of two beats! But then, perhaps sensing that this made some dizzy, it decided to settle in a D Major an octave lower in the second measure. The first part of the tune, measures #1-8, has this overriding theme; that of moving away from D Major only to return to it rather quickly. One gets the impression that the ice is thin everywhere except around D Major.

The second part, measure #9-24, however, takes a slightly different approach. This section begins and ends in D Major, yet, all that falls within is basically centered around A Major. Measure #9, in some respects is the exact opposite of the first measure. Instead of ascending, here it descends to resolve into A Major in measure #10. The 10th-12th measures are overwhelmingly centered around this chord also. Measure #13 goes through a series of chord changes to resolve again to A Major in the next measure. The same theme is repeated in measures #14-16 – that of going through chord progressions of a measure or two only to resolve to a high A Major. The paths they take are quite different but the objective is both the same.

To reemphasize the fact that this section is ruled by A Major it traversed its territory from a low A Major to a high one all in one beat in the 17th measure. It continued to reign in the next measure as well. Measure #19 is very interesting. Vertical block chords go from E minor to B7 then to E Major in the following measure. The very last phrase, measures #21-24 is very reflective and is often repeated to provide for a good ending cadence.

Where in the first section it was cautious not to move far from D Major, the second has the very same feel but with A Major. It may stray, but it is never too far away. The tune has many interesting harmonies. There are many, many instances of very gradual resolutions – chords gently and cautiously creeping in and out of each other. Here we see a number of unusual chords being used in this regard. A7 (with added 2nd) is used to resolve to D Major in the 3rd, 4th, 9th and 15th measures, while B♭7 is seen in a similar situation in the 5th measure. A7 is used in measure #21, while the 13th measure uses C♯ minor in a similar way.

One notices that many 7 chords are employed. This is an example of the experimental atmosphere of the times where we see the newer theory interacting with the older. I would say the experiment was a success. Besides their avante garde chords one finds what one would expect to find in a D Major piece. Yet, the tune cannot decide between E minor and E Major. B7 is used to resolve to E Major in measure #19, while B minor is seen in only one spot – measure #22.

The piece makes use of good effects as well. Note the ascending run in measures #15-16 and the vertical block transition of E minor to its major in measures #19-20. The opening ascension catches one's attention, while the surreal chordal uncertainties give it depth. 16th-note flurries are not placed haphazard but rather strategic. Absolutely the best.

A Galliarde

D Major

Anthony Holborne
(English)

Chordal

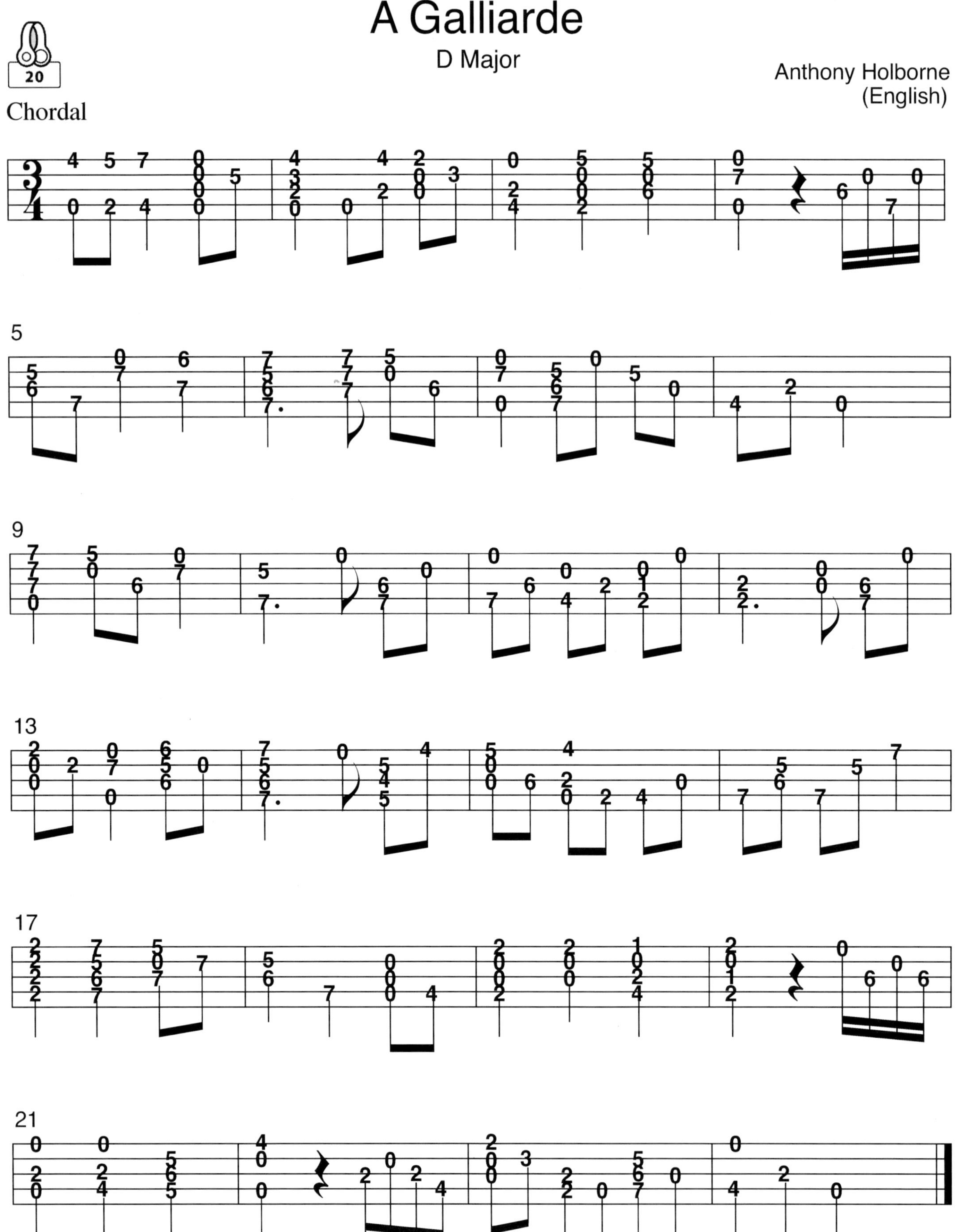

A Galliarde

D Major

Anthony Holborne
(English)

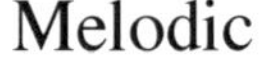

25

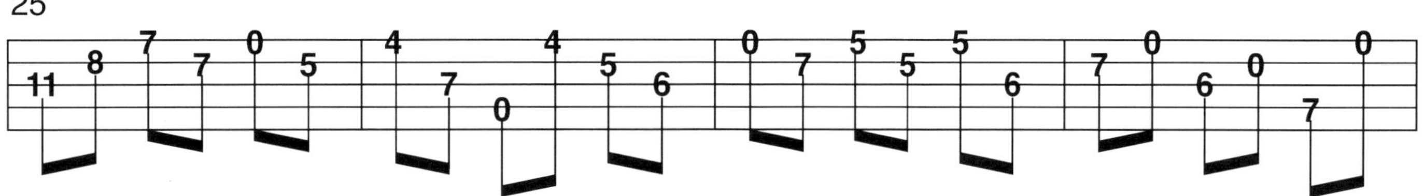

29

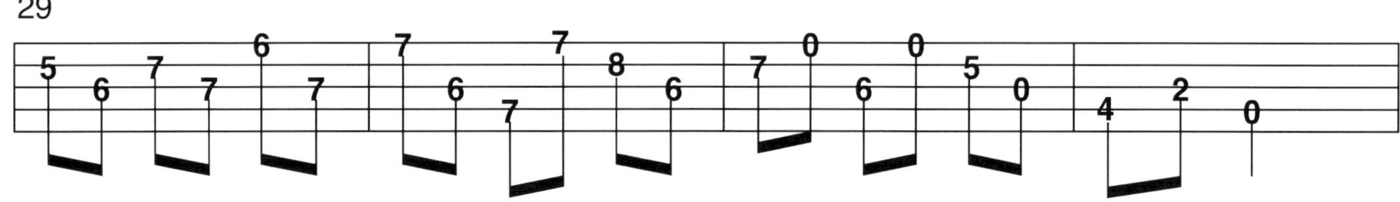

33

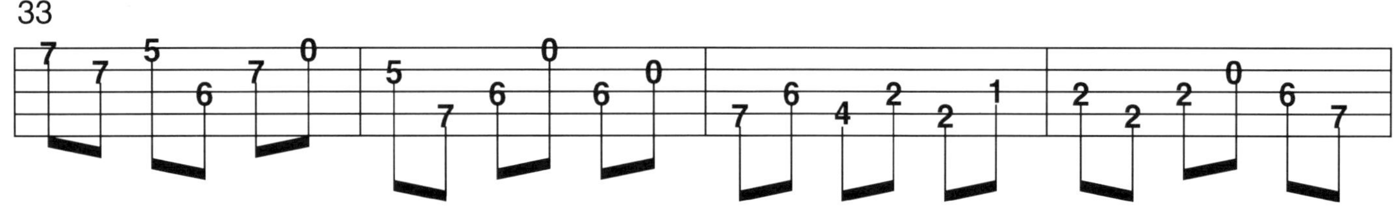

37

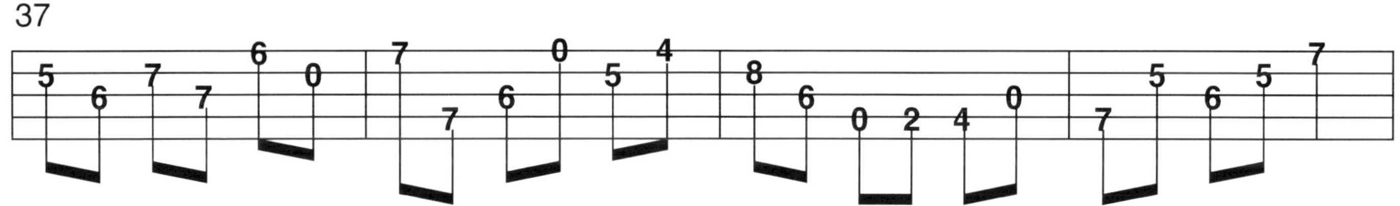

41

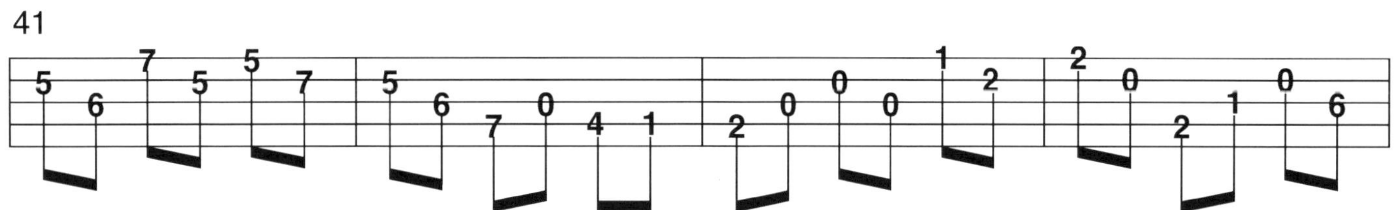

45

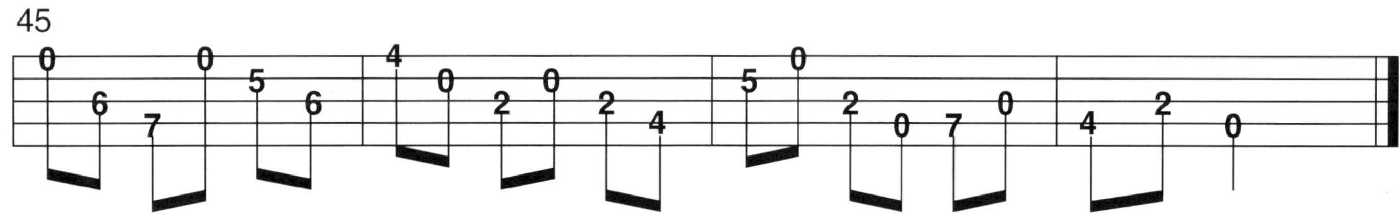

Tutti Venite Armati (Italian)

This is a very short work which may have evolved out of an instructional exercise. It has a very upbeat feel overall. Even the pauses in the 2nd and 6th measures cannot impart a fatalistic aura. The piece is in C Major and so makes much use of G Major and F Major. D Major is encountered in measure #3 where it is used to resolve to G Major. A minor is also used in this particular resolution. Measure #7 presents an interesting ending, using first F Major to A minor, then strangely E minor resolving into the tonic key C Major. This piece would sound excellent in a brass ensemble and could possibly have been a type of fanfare originally for it certainly does have a haughty, noble quality about it.

Tutti Venite Armati

C Major

(Italian)

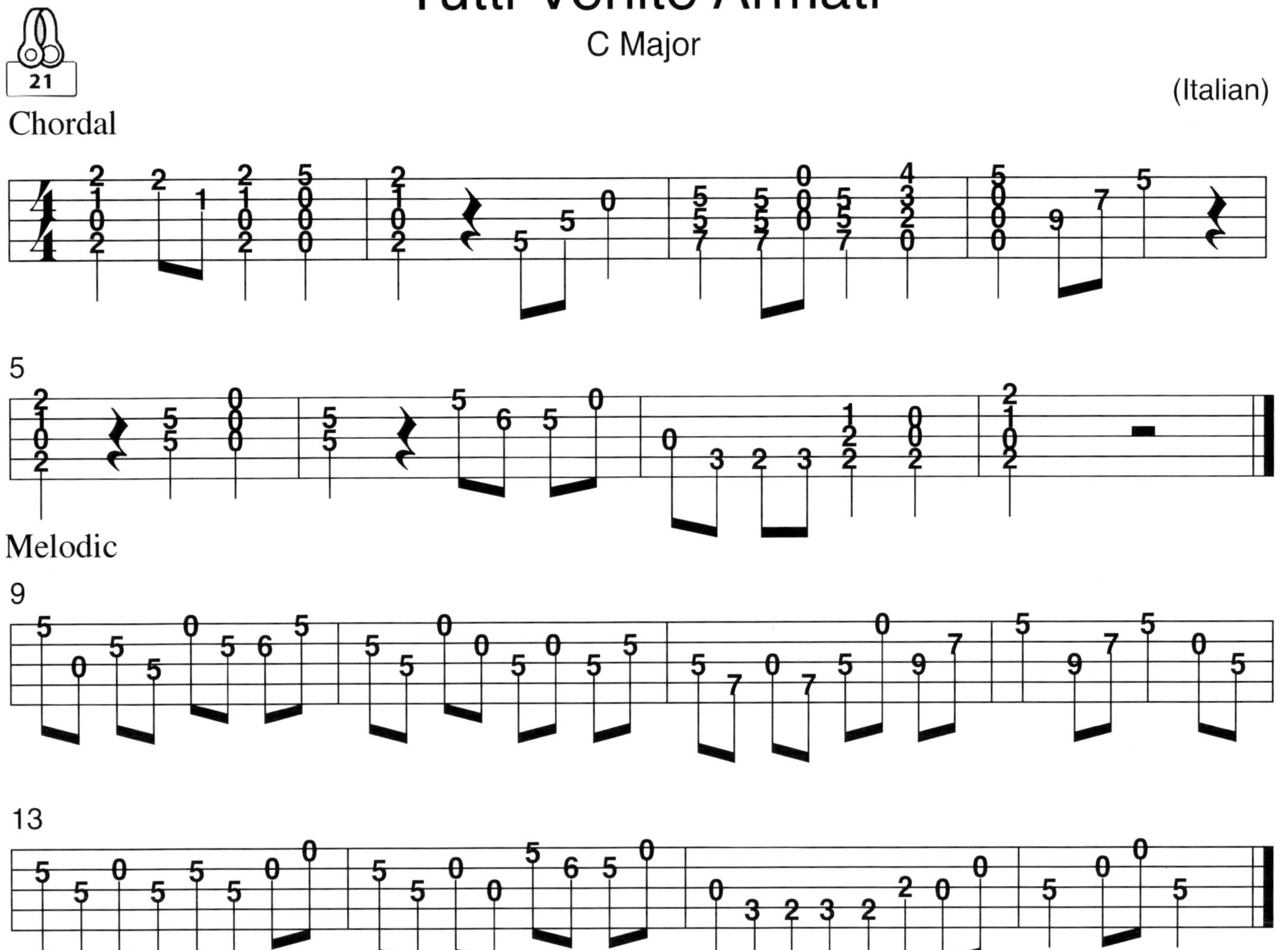

Gagliarda Nova (Italian)

The title of this tune is very appropriate for it translated as the "new Galliarde." It shows how some of the new tonalities were being merged with the old modal scales. The beginning of this work is similar to that of Besarde's Galliarde as they both go from a low A minor to a high G note, here incorporated into a high E minor chord. There the similarity ends for following this optimistic high point is a depressing B♭ Major chord with an F Major and then C Major right behind. The piece remains low-key for the next two measures in G Major until it resolves to A Major endings in measures #8 and 16. The endings in measures #7 and 15 are very interesting as they use some unusual chords. F Major goes to an A Major (with added 2nd) and then A♭ Major before coming to rest on A Major. Measure #11 presents an interesting chord for this work – a B7 chord. This was a very modern sounding chord for the time, and lends credence to the title of the piece. It is used to resolve to an E Major chord in the 12th measure. The rapid-strum technique, common in Renaissance Italian music is seen in the 13th measure, going from E Major to A minor. The technique was one which was common during this period but was preserved only through the music of the Spanish. It is used to try to emphasize the resolved E Major chord of measure #12. This eventually fails as the piece ends up, in Renaissance fashion, in the major of the minor key it started out in. It is a transition piece, one which shows that the Baroque period is near at hand.

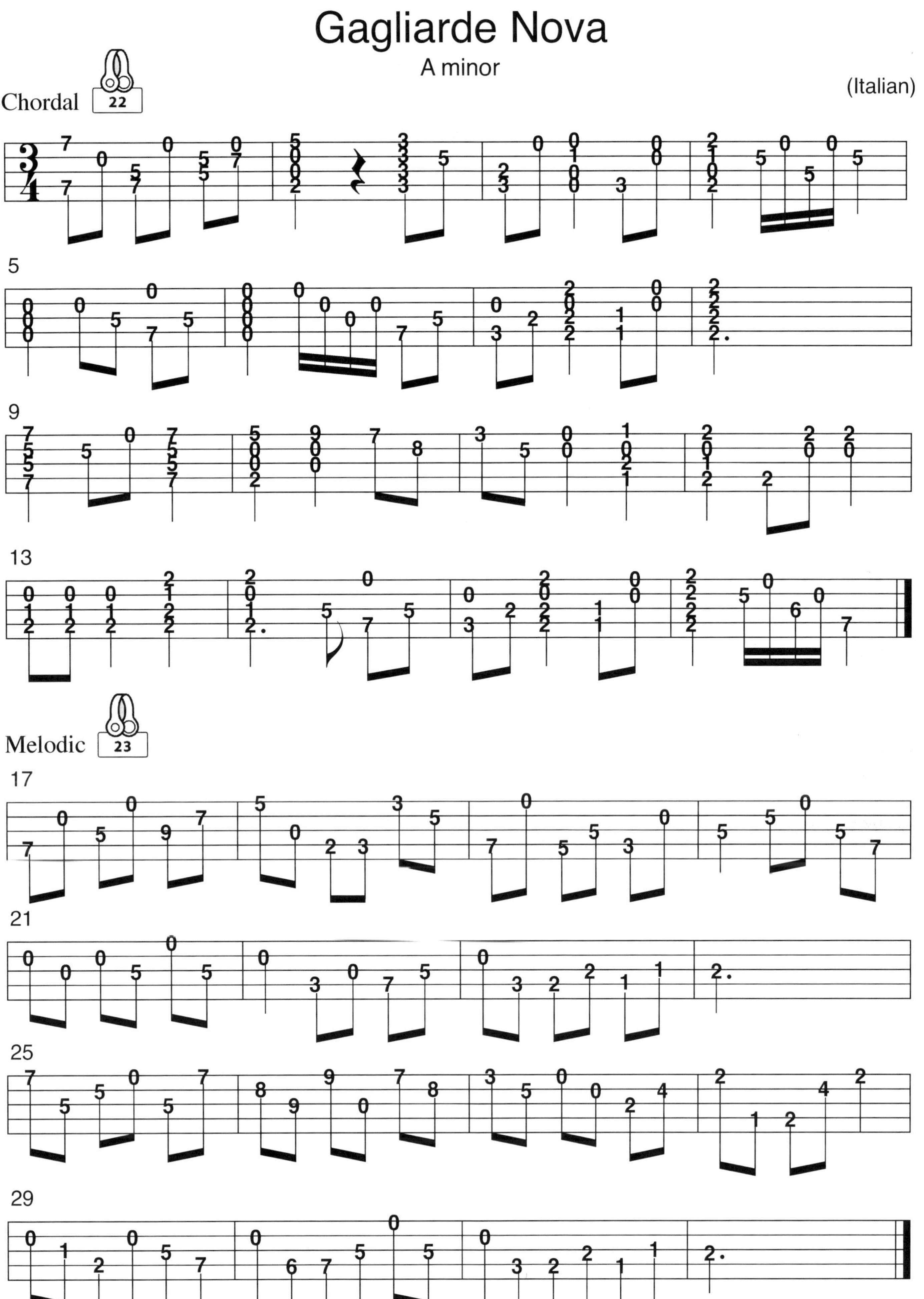
Gagliarde Nova
A minor
(Italian)
Chordal
22
Melodic
23

Fiamenga (Italian)

"Fiamenga" is a good example of a thorough-composed piece that is not overly-sophisticated. None of its parts are repeated although measures #5-8 do resemble the first phrase somewhat. Yet the rest of the work is all new unrepeated material. Measures #9-12 present an entirely new musical statement. The 13th and 14th measures suggest an entirely new thought. It is then subsequently doubted by the following two measures which add its own idea, similar but different enough to be considered a replacement. Measure #17 rejects both preceding ideas and the A minor chord begins a nihilistic mood which lasts for the rest of the piece.

Overall, there is a feeling of much conflict. Conflict among the different musical ideas which seem to want to oust each other. Even though the tune ends in a major key, pessimism has its way as the last idea to be offered has an obvious mournful feel to it.

This is another one of those tunes which ends in a key different, but related, to the one it began in. It begins in A minor but ends in D Major. This along with the fact that it is thorough-composed gives the composer the chance to use a wide variety of chords. Thus we find many different ones yet all being closely related to either A minor or D Major. The only possible exception being the G minor chord in measures #13 and 18. But it is specifically the use of a foreign tonality which suggests a new idea beginning in measure #13. Unusual chords can be used to express departure from the norm or as an anti-thesis – so this is to be expected. Unusual chords can also be used during a transition when one chord is turning into another. An example here is in measure #3 where an A Major (with added 2nd) is sandwiched between an F Major and an E Major. It makes for a much more interesting transformation. 16th-note flurries are used in the 4th measure to emphasize an A Major chord and in the 6th measure to help wind down a G Major scale passage.

Fiamenga

A minor

(Italian)

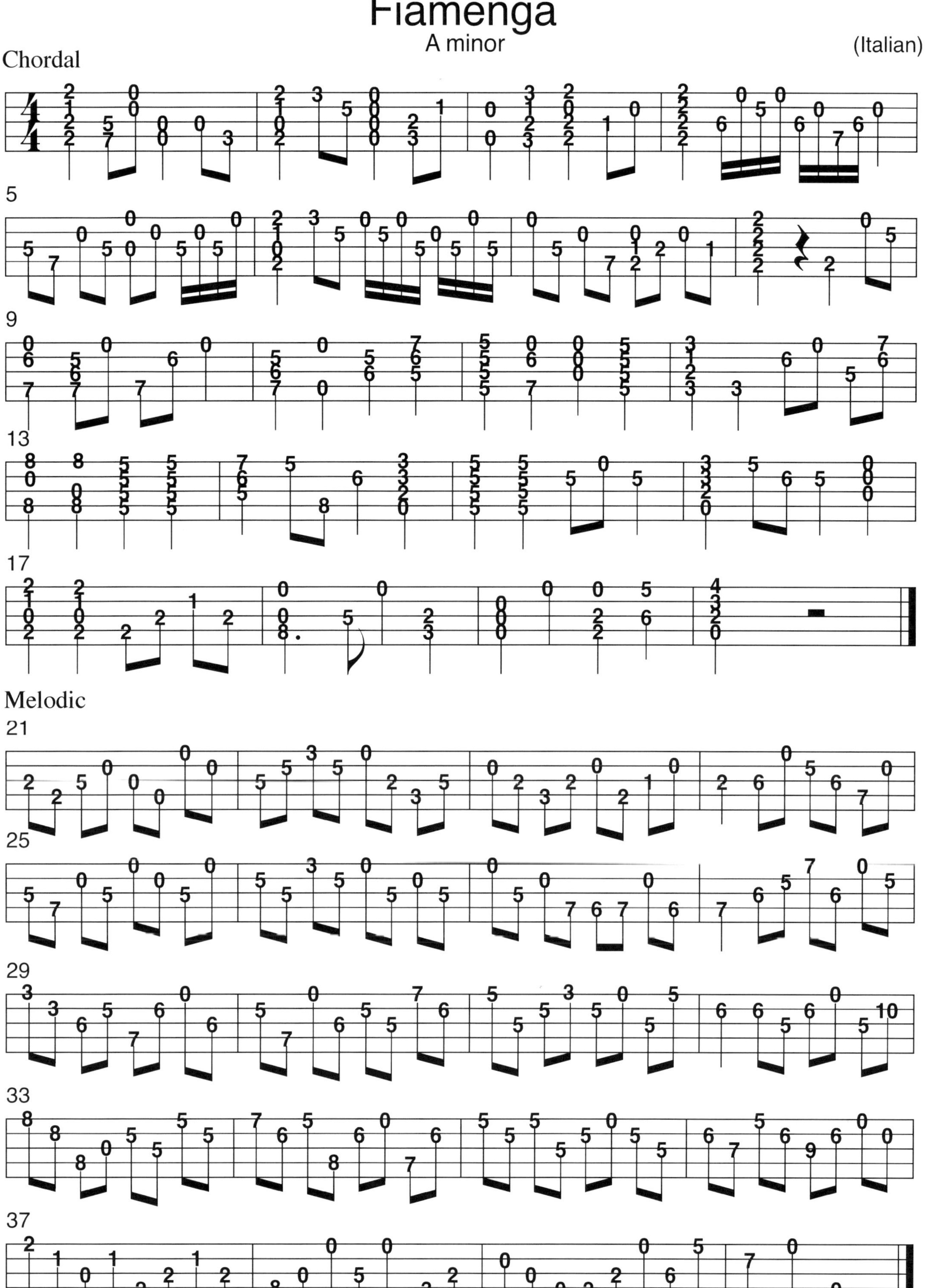

Canzona - fieri ochi "He has fire in his eyes" (Italian)

This work is fantastic. The title indicates that it has to do with fire in your cousin's eyes. I had heard it long before I was able to play it. It is a Canzona, which in Italian means "song," and this is reflected in its structure. Instead of the symmetrical dance form it has a few measures extra. This adds much to the song for these additional measures are very pleasing. The reason I like this work so much is that it flows so nicely. Even the vertical block chords, which usually would have a tendency to fragment, cannot interrupt this flow. It is as if its progression is inevitable. The ending of its first part begs to be continued in the second. This incessant plodding is even more apparent when the piece is presented a second time in the linear perpetual motion style.

The tonic key is presented in the first measure, and then proceeds to ascend very rapidly in the second. In these first two measures there is little to suggest continuity, but in the third the beginning of this overpowering flow is felt. The remainder of the first part is this chordal progression unwinding itself. In this sense the tune reminds one of a clock. The first measure presents the reality that you are dealing with a clock. In the second measure it is being wound up very tightly. In fact, going from completely unwound, the low E Major chord, all the way to fully wound, which is represented by the high G Major. This all happens in the space of only one measure, which is a relatively short time. Compared to the actual running of a clock (its unwinding) the amount of time required to wind it up is also very, very short. Measures #3-10 can be compared to the long gradual unwinding of the clock. It winds back down to the same low register, here an A Major, in which it started out unwound. The analogy is perfect.

The piece starts in A minor but ends up in A Major, so naturally E Major is found in abundance. D minor which is what one normally finds in the key of A minor has been replaced by its relative major, F Major. G Major is seen quite often, C Major somewhat less so. For such a short piece, it has its share of the more unusual chords. G7 is found in the fifth measure, while A minor (with an added 6th) is seen in the fourth. A Major (with added 2nd) is used in the endings of each section where it acts as a catalyst between other chords. This seems to be a common function for it in Renaissance cadences and endings.

Canzone - Fieri Ochi

A minor

(Italian)

Chordal

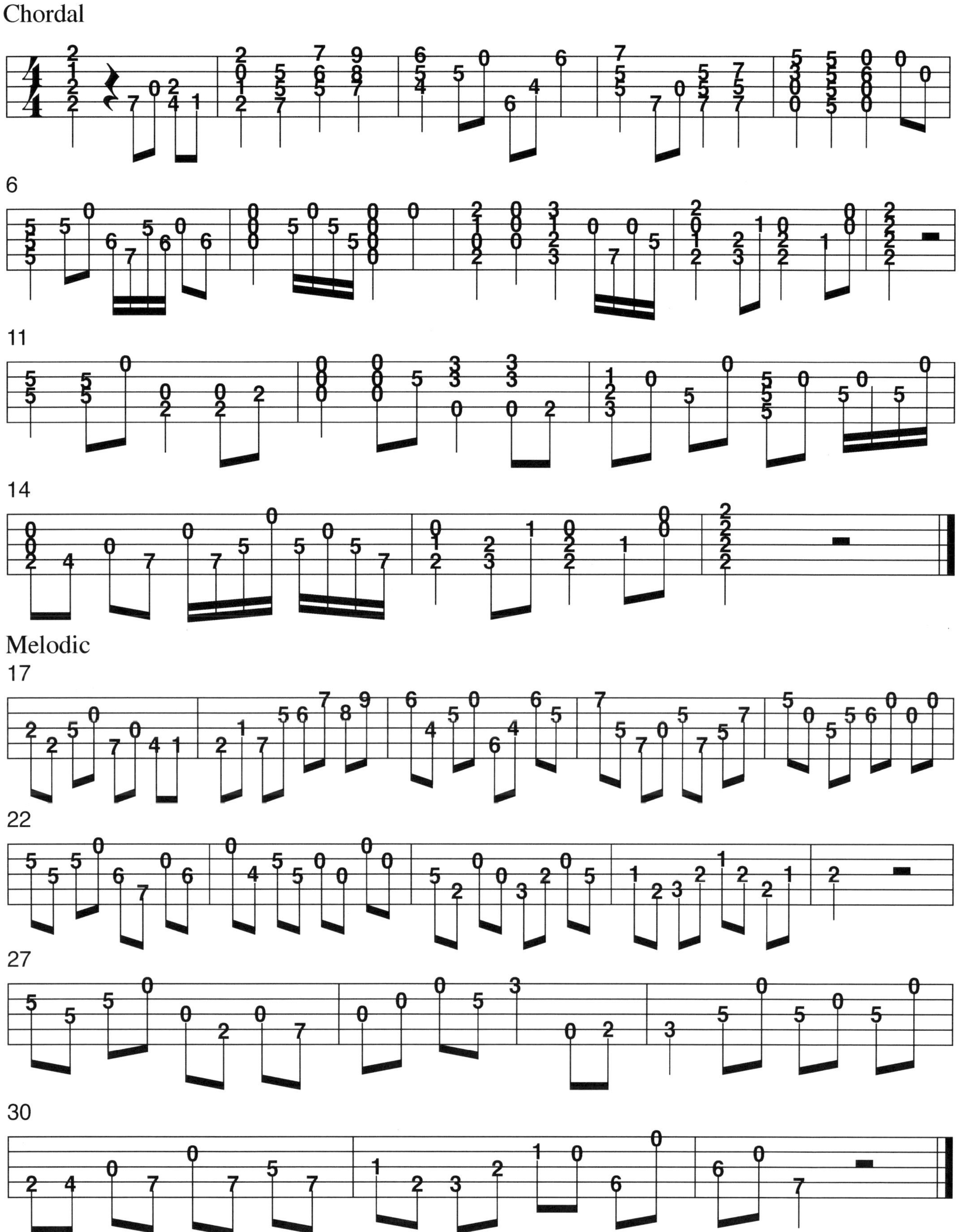

Fantasia (Italian)

This is a nice example of a free form. Generally speaking, it begins in a high register and then gradually sinks. The first eight measures show this as it descends from a high B note down to an E minor chord. Measures 9-12 then take a small step upward to an E minor chord an octave higher. Measures #13-16 and #17-20 both show different ways to resolve to a low E minor chord, where measures #21-25 show a final resolution to E minor. Measures #25-32 are a repeat of the first eight measures. The last seven measures make a final resolution to the tonic key – E minor.

Being in E minor the piece naturally uses relative chords such as A minor. Interestingly enough, both B Major and B minor are found although the B Major a bit more often as it is used extensively to resolve to the tonic. G Major, the relative major of E minor, is often encountered. In fact, it began with this chord. D Major makes rare appearances in measures #3, 27, 34, and 35. The most unusual chord that shows up is the F♯ minor chord which is used here to move into a B Major chord.

Some fantasies are smooth flowing melodic works, while others like this one sound very choppy and exhibit a march-like quality.

Fantasia

E minor

(Italian)

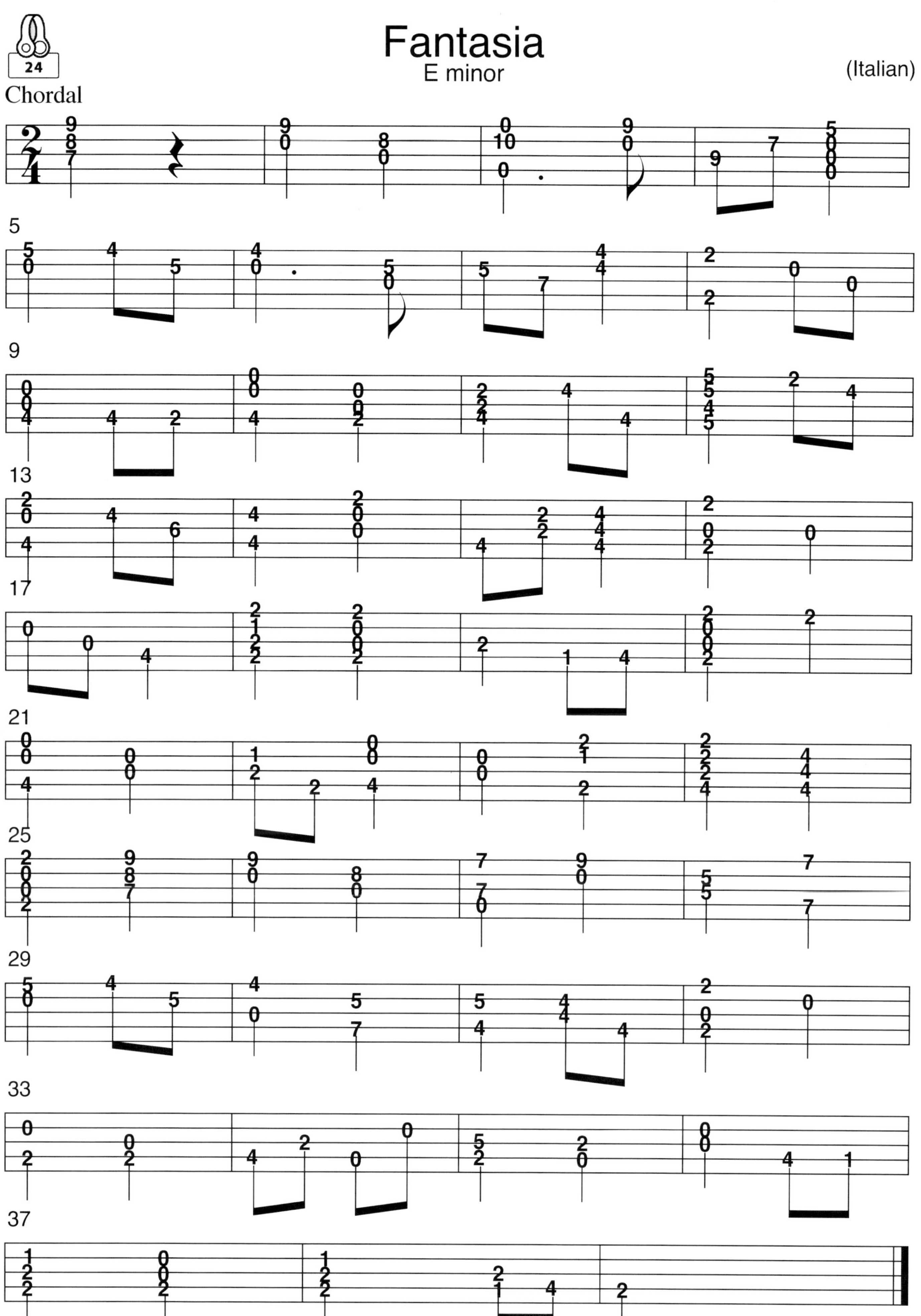

Melodic

Fantasia

E minor

(Italian)

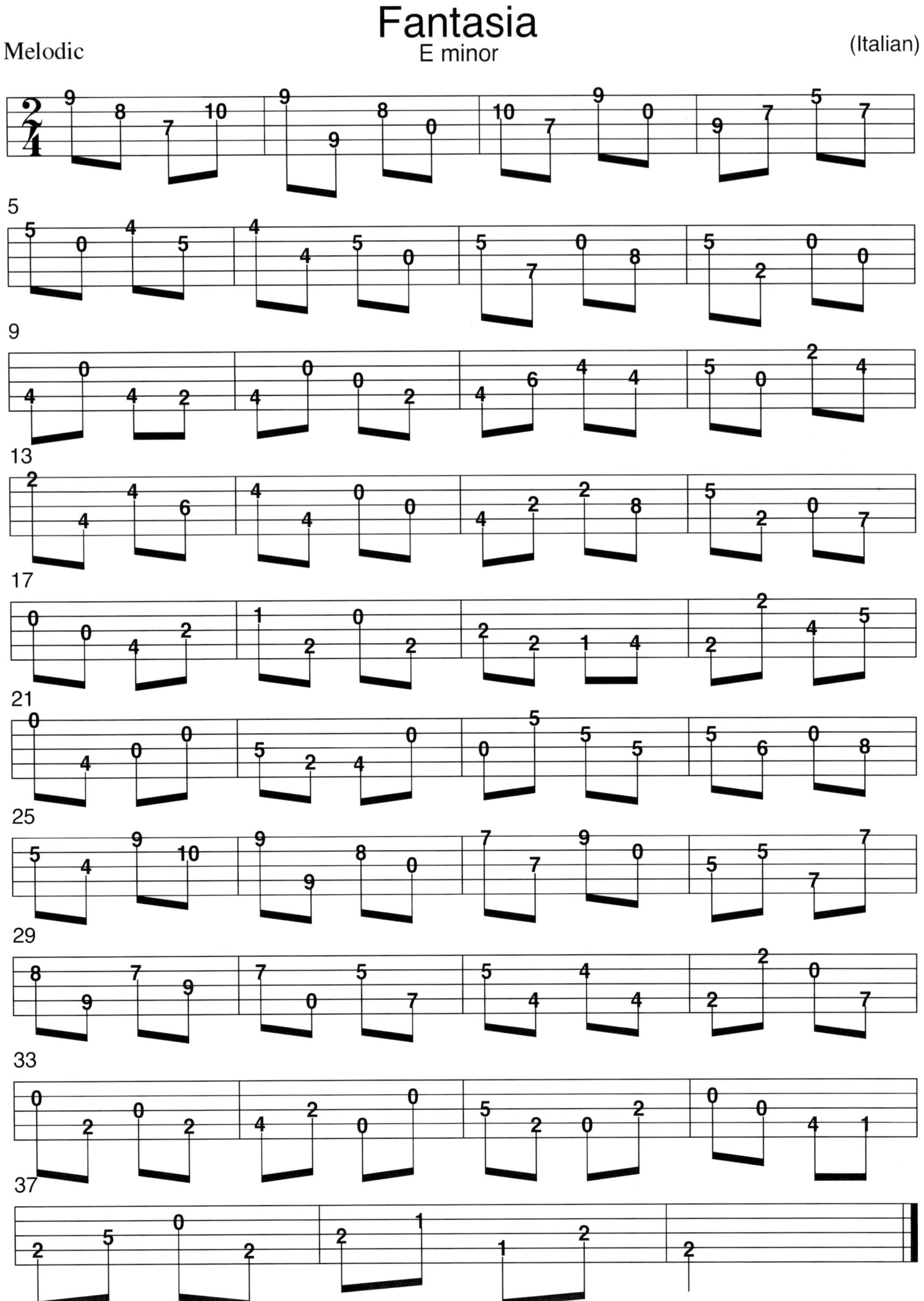

Spagnolletta - "Spanish Dance" (Italian/Spanish)

This is one of those pieces, which is written by an Italian imitating a Spaniard. Is it then Italian or Spanish?? Nevertheless, it is a very interesting work since it is thorough-composed and in an unusual key, B minor. It is also one of those strange tunes which can be uplifting if played fast or equally depressing if rendered slow.

The tune slowly ascends from a B minor beginning to a high D Major in the beginning of the 5th measure. It then descends to a low D Major in measures #6-8. The first phrase is then repeated in measures #9-12. A statement is made in A Major and E minor in its next two measures, then in B minor in the 15th, which then resolves into a F♯ Major fantasy which lasts for practically the remainder of the tune. The only real change of mood in the tune comes about in measures #19-21 when F♯ Major makes its presence known.

Since the piece is in B minor, A Major and D Major are common throughout. G Major should be and is also found. Somewhat more rare is its relative minor, E minor, found only in measures #19 & 21. F♯ Major makes its debut in the 16th measure but has little impact until it drives its point home in the 19th measure. B Major shows up unexpectedly and unannounced in the nice little cadence in measure #17. The cadence is used again for the ending. A very rarely encountered chord, G♯ minor, is used in measures #18 and 20 to lead into the F♯ Major. This is a piece which is relatively easy in theory, yet in practice may prove difficult due to the unusual fingering.

Spagnolletta

B minor

(Italian/Spanish)

33

Chordal

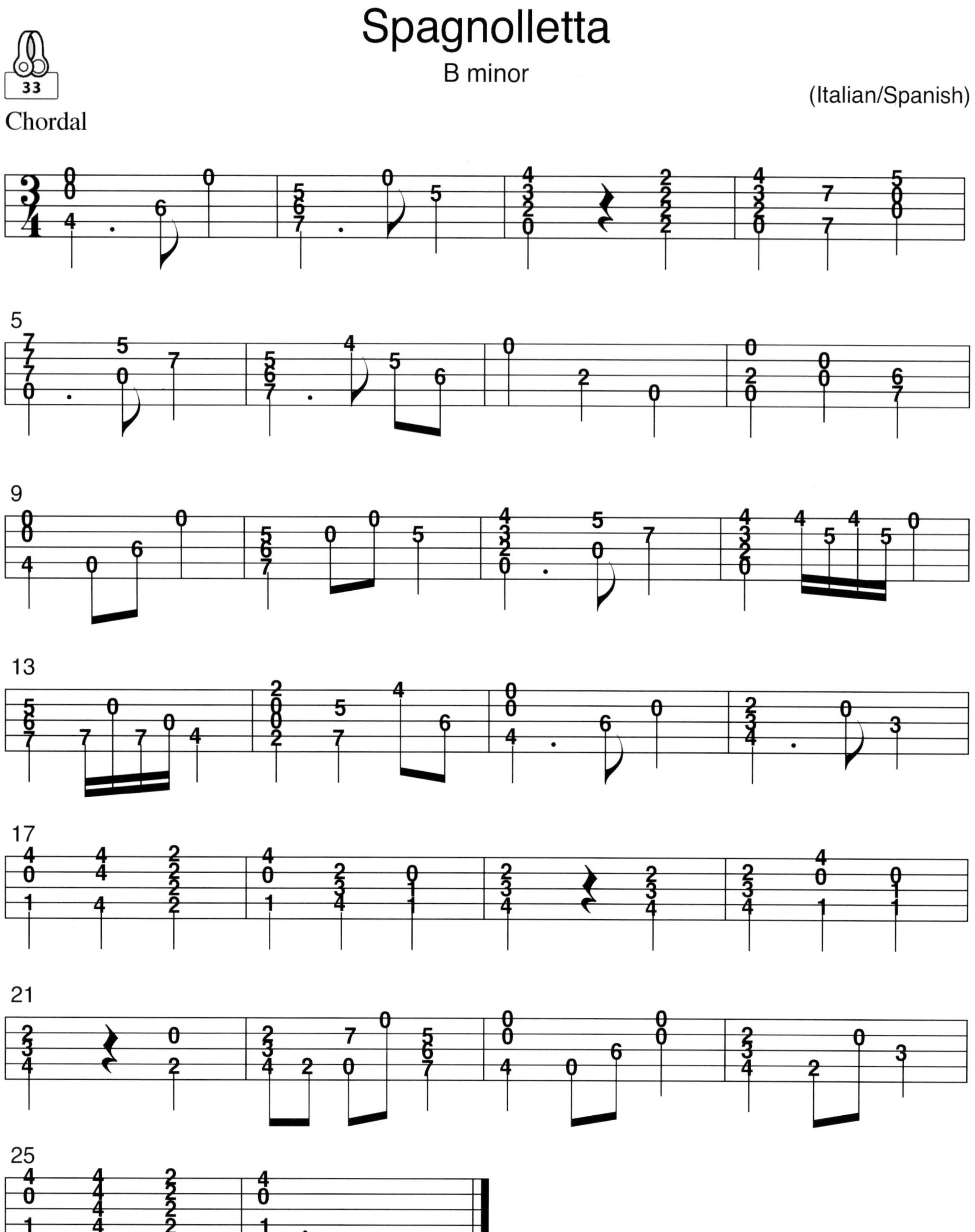

Spagnolletta

B minor

(Italian/Spanish)

Melodic

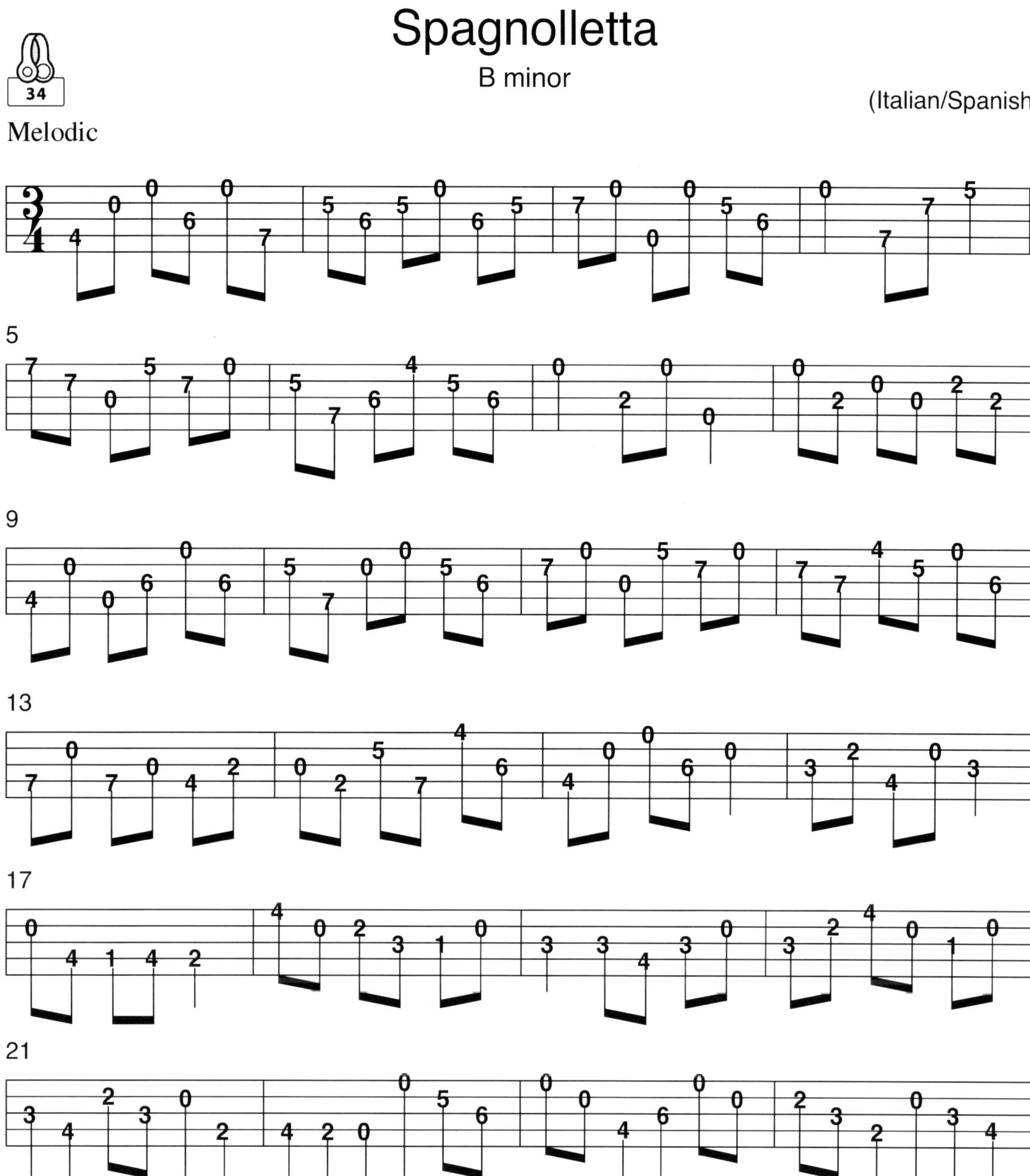

This page has been left blank to avoid awkward page turns.

Fabrito Caruso (1580)
A Villanella (Italian)

This Villanella is probably the most played piece in my repertoire. Simplicity in theory and fingering and its stately air are some of the reasons why. I like to play it at weddings when a promenade is called for. I happened to learn the tune from a fellow musician at a Renaissance Fair.

Villanellas were light, easy dance tunes which were probably derived from folk music. This one is comprised of three sections of eight measures each. What gives the piece its charm is the way many of the notes are syncopated which gives it a pleasing, jumpy feel. The work is strophic, yet the second time a phrase is repeated it is elaborated. Quarter-note strums give it a strong march-like quality.

The piece is in E Major yet each section has its dominating chord – the first section has D Major, the second A Major, and the third C Major. The first section has a very stately feel to it. It is in D Major and uses an E minor instead of an A Major for resolutions. This gives it a much more modal flavor. The second section is dominated by A Major, which uses G Major chords again giving it a modal, in this instance, Dorian, character. The last section is controlled by the C Major chords which interplay with the tonic key – D Major.

The way in which the sections contrast each other was intentional as this was a common dynamic device. The first part is stately and uplifting while the second offers another, more pessimistic perspective. The first phrase of the third part seems to want to back away from the melancholy, and certainly does so in the last phrase of the last section. One of the best tunes.

Villanella

D Major

Fabrito Caruso
(Italian)

Chordal

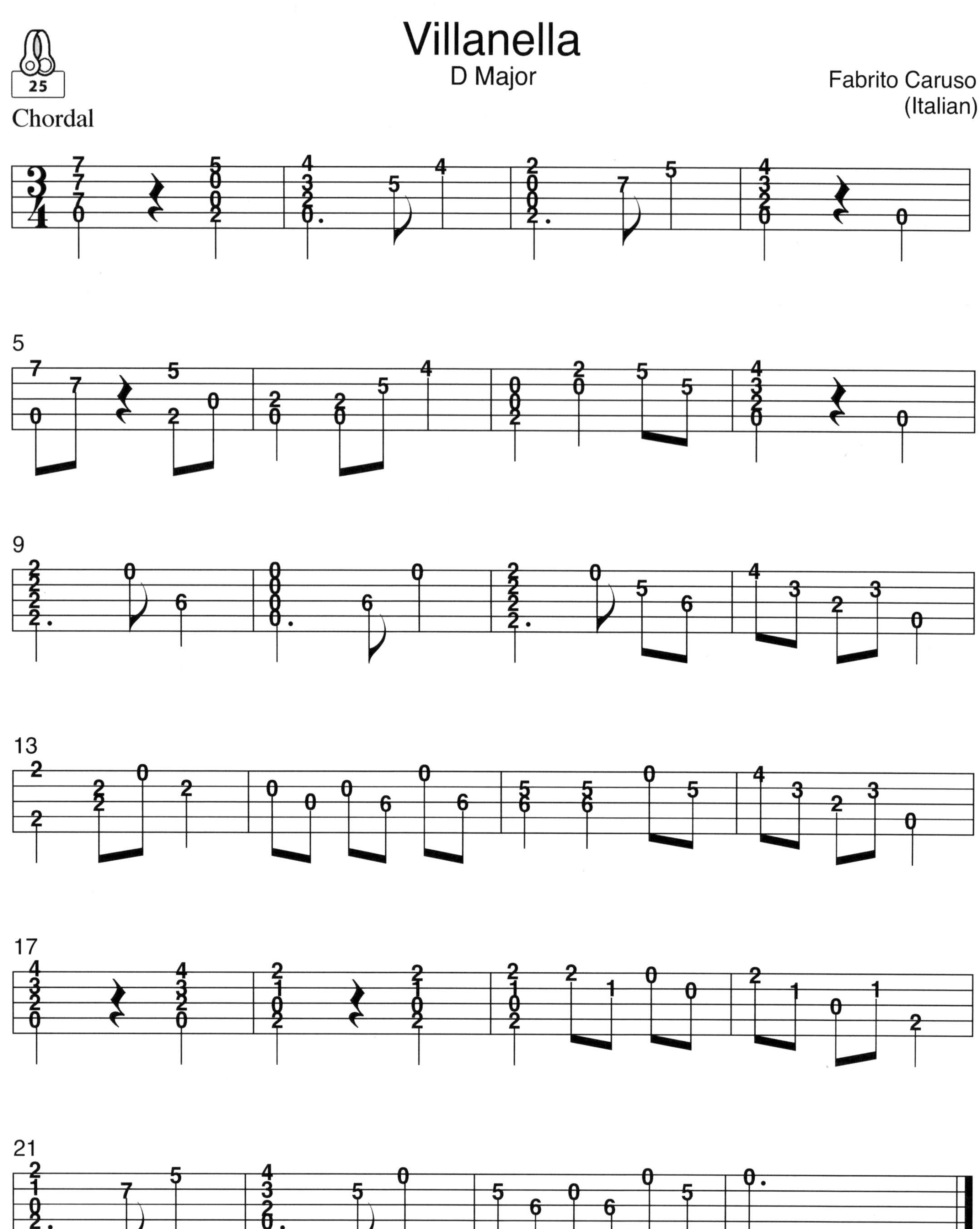

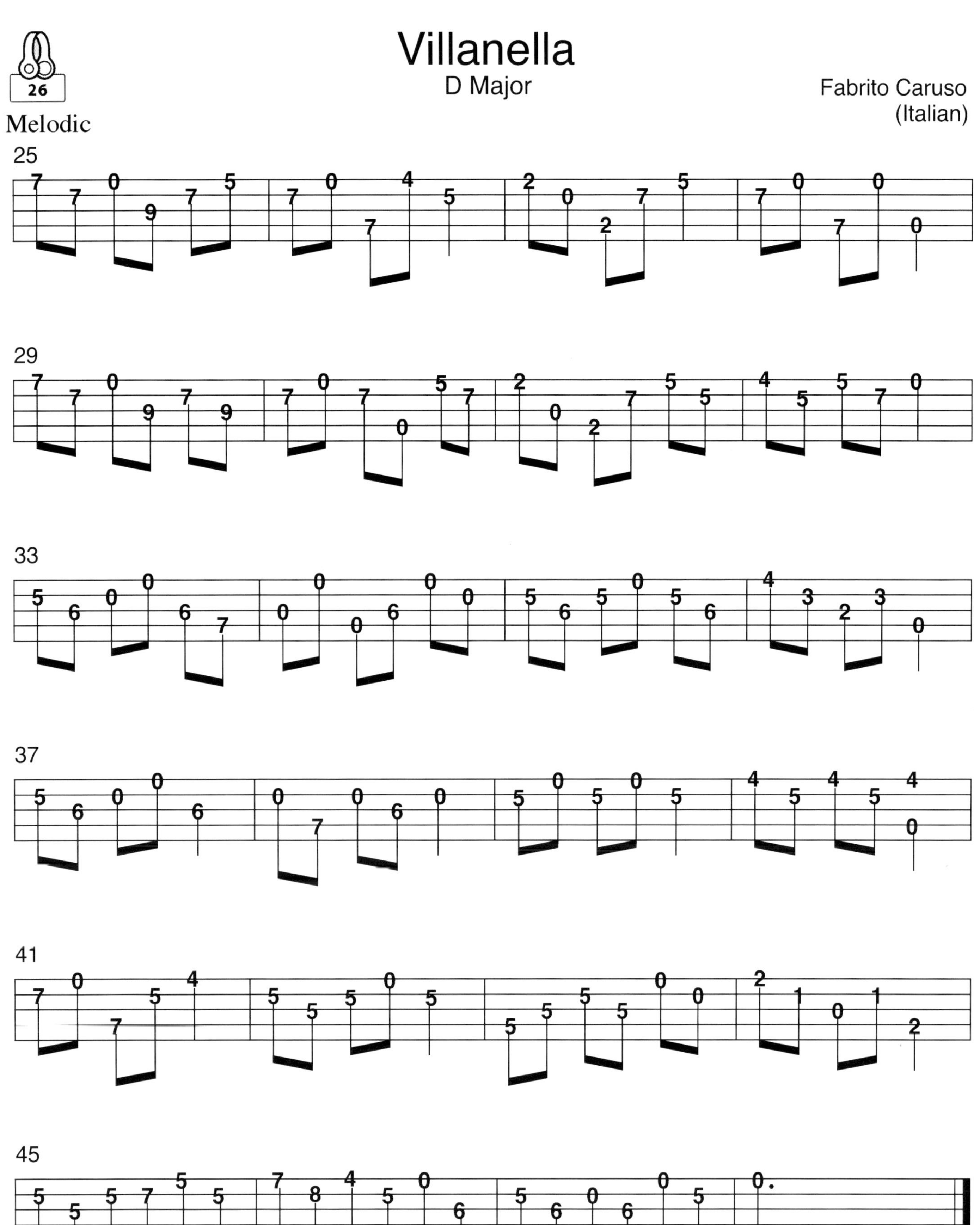

26
Melodic
Villanella
D Major
Fabrito Caruso
(Italian)

Caesare Negri (1546-1609)
Gagliarda/Pavaniglia #1 (Italian)

All of these dances by Caesare Negri are related in form and style. They are good examples of Galiarde/Pavaniglia pairing. The first dance is in triple time while its mate is in duple. The Gagliarda is a superb example of uptempo Italian music. If forced upon it, the Gagliarda can be played somberly although this usually does not last for long. The syncopated rhythm throughout causes the player to find himself speeding up considerably. Ventures into the higher registers in measures #5, 9 and 13 keeps it fresh.

The Gagliarda is in E Major, yet B Major is found sparingly, only in the first and second to last measures. Much more common are D Major, which is understandable, and G Major, which is not. In the second measure, E Major turns into E minor and so this is probably how the G Major fits in. In the second section A Major shows up finally in measures #10, 11 & 15.

The second dance of this pair, the Pavaniglia is characteristically much more moody. The first phrase, measures #1-4 states a depressing musical thought and is followed by the next four measures by an alternative thought which is equally pessimistic. Measures #9-12 seem to be pensively analyzing the preceding statements. The ninth measure begins with an A Major and ends with the same, perhaps indicating that no conclusion had been reached since things had stayed the same. This is particularly true of the eleventh measure where it can be seen that there is much activity within the measure yet it takes the listener nowhere. Measure #11 is a run in E Major which had just broken away from an A Major simply to find itself in its clutches again beginning in the next measure. One gets the feeling that measure #11 was all in vain. Optimism shows its face very briefly in the 13th and 14th measures only to be shown false in the 15th.

This Pavaniglia shows the reverse of what usually goes on in music of this period. Here the piece begins in a major key, D Major, and then ends, not in its minor, D minor, but rather its relative minor, B minor. This is encountered occasionally. What also makes it fascinating is that sometimes B Major replaces B minor. This is seen in the 4th and 9th measures. As the tune is in D Major, G Major and A Major are found throughout. C Major makes an unusual appearance in the third measure while F♯ Major is used in measures #7 and 8 to lead into a B Major and in the 15th measure to resolve into the B minor ending.

Gagliarda/Pavaniglia #1

E Major/D Major

Caesare Negri
(Italian)

Chordal

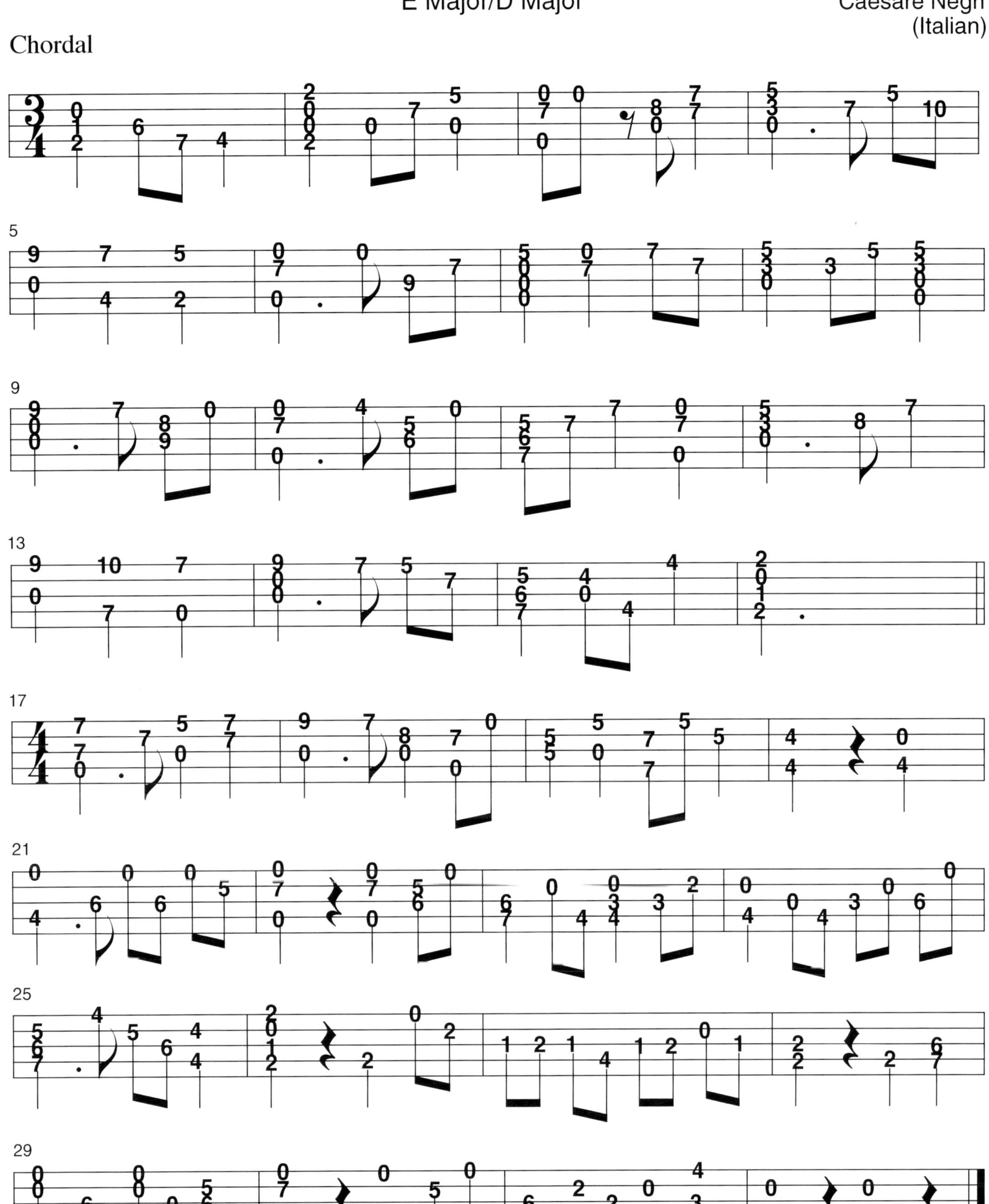

Gagliarda/Pavaniglia #1

E Major/D Major

Caesare Negri
(Italian)

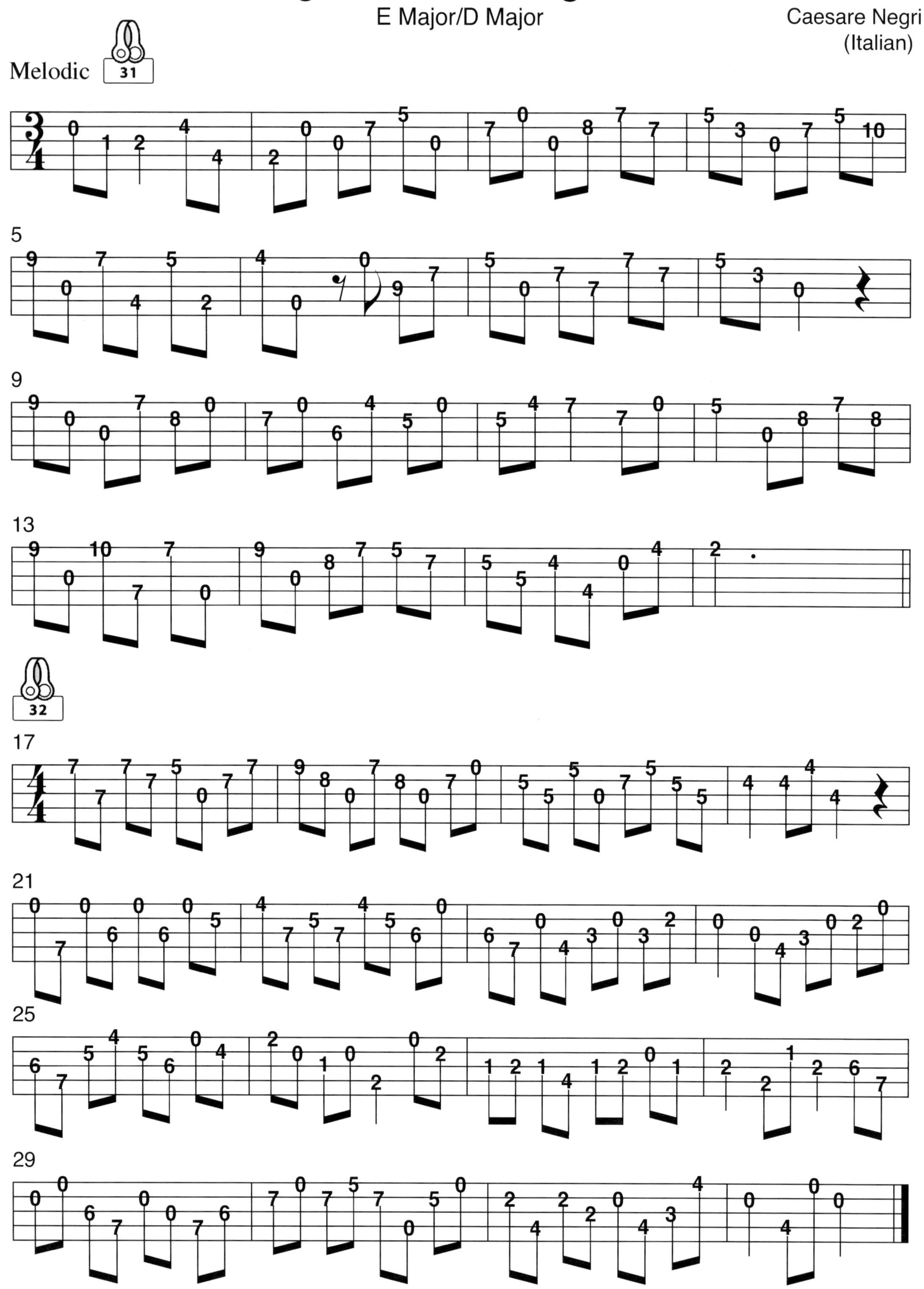

Caesare Negri (1546-1604)
Gagliarda/Pavaniglia #2 (Italian)

This second paired dance by Mr. Negri is similar to the first. The Gagliarda is very festive in nature. Any pessimism that may be present (it is hinted at in measures #10-12) is quickly eliminated. The last phrase, measures #13-16 are very very optimistic and the 16th-note flurry in the 14th measure adds to this euphoria. The first part is entirely strophic while the second is less so. The vertical block strums in the 1st and 9th-11th measures are very typical of Italian celebratory music.

Like the preceding paired dance the Gagliarda begins in D Major and ends in its relative minor, B minor. As most of it is in D Major, G Major and A Major are used extensively. E minor shows up in the 11th and 13th measures. In the first phrase, measures #1-4, the statement resolves to B minor, where in the second, measures #5-8, the identical phrase resolves into a D Major. Measures #9-11 show block strums where only syncopation saves them from monotony. Syncopation is also used throughout which helps give it a joyous sub-alpine feeling. The work is very straightforward without any foreign elements. Only the E minor strums in the 11th measure show any slight hint at deviance.

The Pavaniglia is much more complex and interesting. It is thorough-composed and exhibits a reverse of key from the Gagliarda. It begins in B minor and ends in its relative major, D Major. It also shows its rebellious nature for it is not as somber as a Pavana is supposed to be. In fact, the last four measures are downright euphoric. Measures #1-3 state a moody message which is punctuated by a descending bass line in the fourth and fifth measures. In measures #5-7, the musical statement is collecting its thoughts, where in measures #7-8 it has decided that things are not so bad after all. This then leads to an explosion of euphoria as measures #9-12 take us on an ascending run which culminates in a 16th-note flurry and the finish.

As the piece wavers between D Major and B minor, it is not surprising to find A Major throughout. G Major had been largely replaced by E minor. Like its sister, the Gagliarda, it is very mainstream with little unexpected.

Gagliarda/Pavaniglia #2

D Major/B minor

Caesare Negri
(Italian)

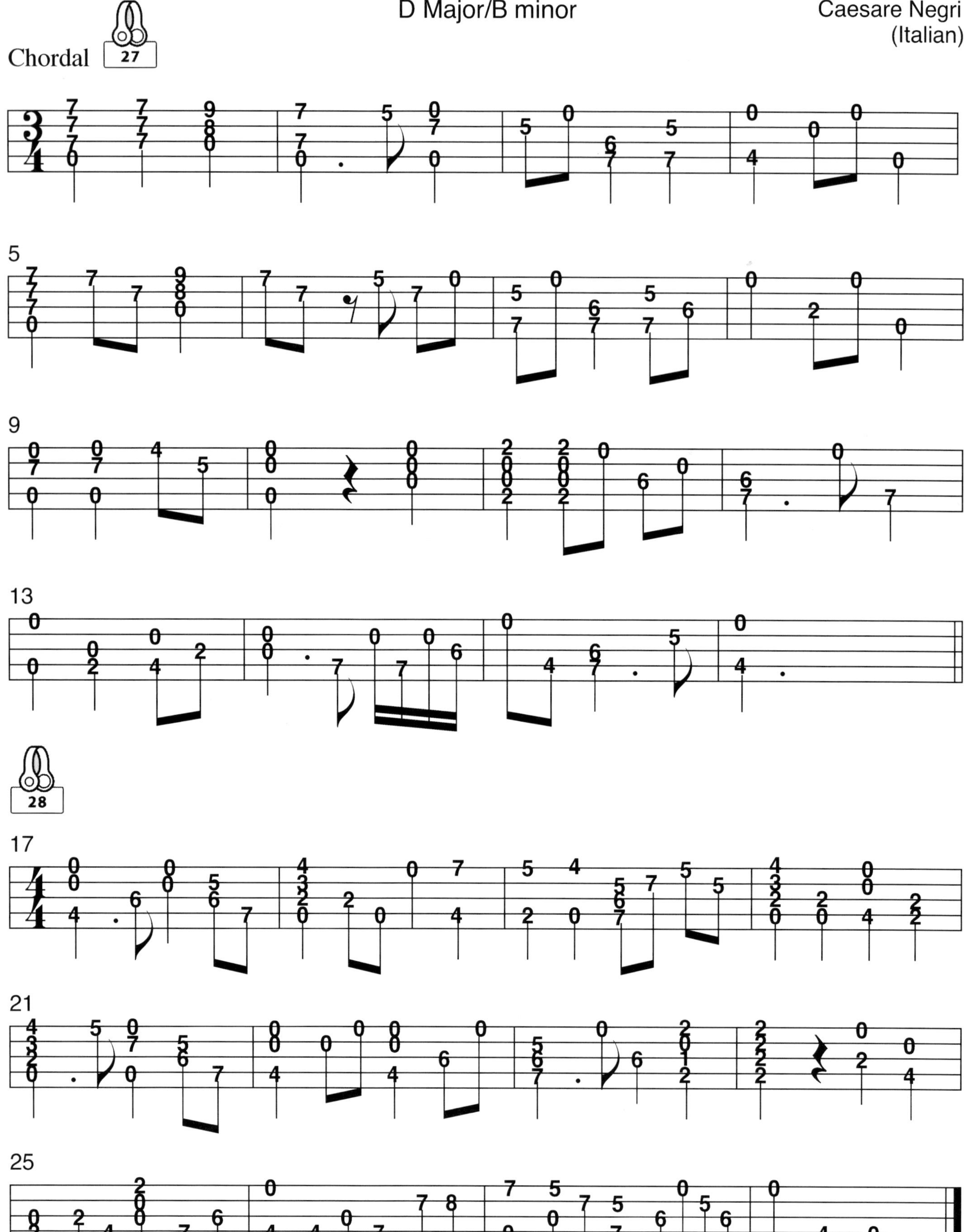

Gagliarda/Pavaniglia #2

D Major/B minor

Caesare Negri
(Italian)

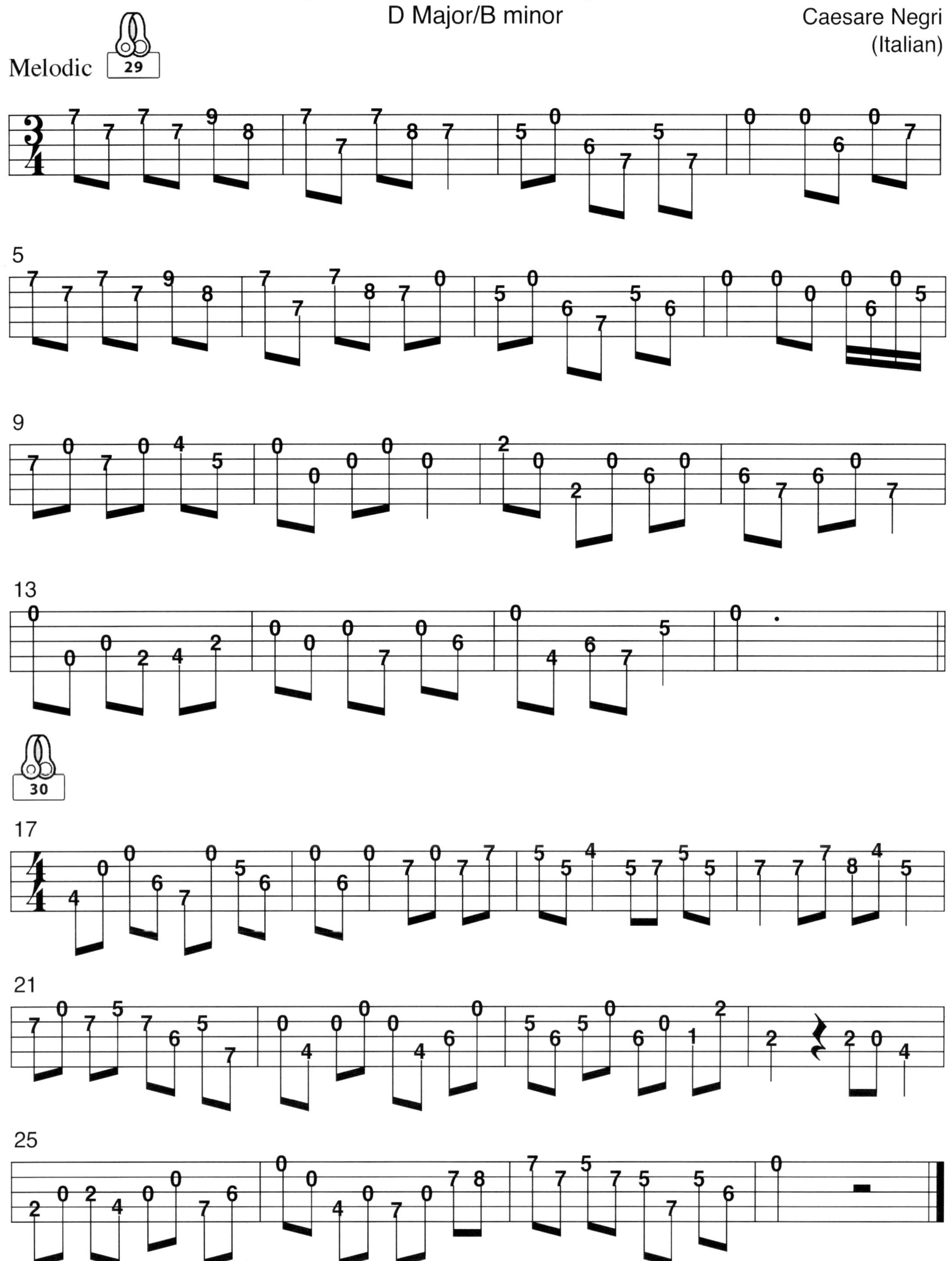

Louis de Narvaez (1530-1550)
Guardame Las Vacas (Spanish)

Another one of my favorites. It is a good example of the form "theme & variations." Every eight measure section is a variation of the first. This is true for all but the last eight measures, which serve as a cadence and ending. "Variations" is found here on an even smaller scale, as the second and sixth measures are variations of the first and fifth. The way that the tune is presented here and the way it was originally played gives it a very haunting, melancholy character. Yet, I suppose if many of the details and nuances are left out, it could be adapted to be a fast-paced dance.

Perhaps the reason it has this dour feel is that one can sense a very slow deathmarch in the background. This was accomplished by the composer assigning one chord for each measure. Each chord is self-contained within its own measure and gives it the sound of a march. As Spain and German areas were united during much of this time, one wonders how much German influence is presented here.

Strangely enough, it could be said to resemble the "country blues" in some respect. In the blues, a short statement is made and then again repeated but in a different key. This is then followed by a conclusion. A similar pattern can be seen here. In the first measure a statement is made in A minor. This is then followed by a slight variation of it but in a different chord, G Major. A conclusion in A minor and then E Major follows. This same sequence is then repeated again in some of the "variations."

The piece is in A minor throughout and makes much use of G Major and E Major. D minor shows up in the cadence near the end. Foreign chords are entirely lacking. Each chord has its own measure which acts as a cellblock. A minor is found in measures #1, 3, 5, 8, 9, 11, 13, 16, 17, 21, 25, 27, 28, and 32. G Major is contained in measures #2, 6, 10, 14 and 19. And E Major is in solitary confinement in measures #4, 7, 12, 15, 18, 20, 22, 23, 24, and 26. Only in the ending cadence do chords interweave together. This creates a faster paced passage which seems to want to get the entire thing over with – and quickly. This is in direct contrast with the rest of the tune, which is in a very cautious mood. One gets the feeling that the piece doesn't want to progress, yet something is pushing it forward. This atmosphere is prevalent throughout until the ending cadence where it rushes forward to the finish line. The piece did not want to be here and when it does arrive it rushes to leave immediately.

Guardame Las Vacas

A minor

Louis de Narvaez
(Spanish)

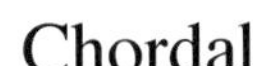

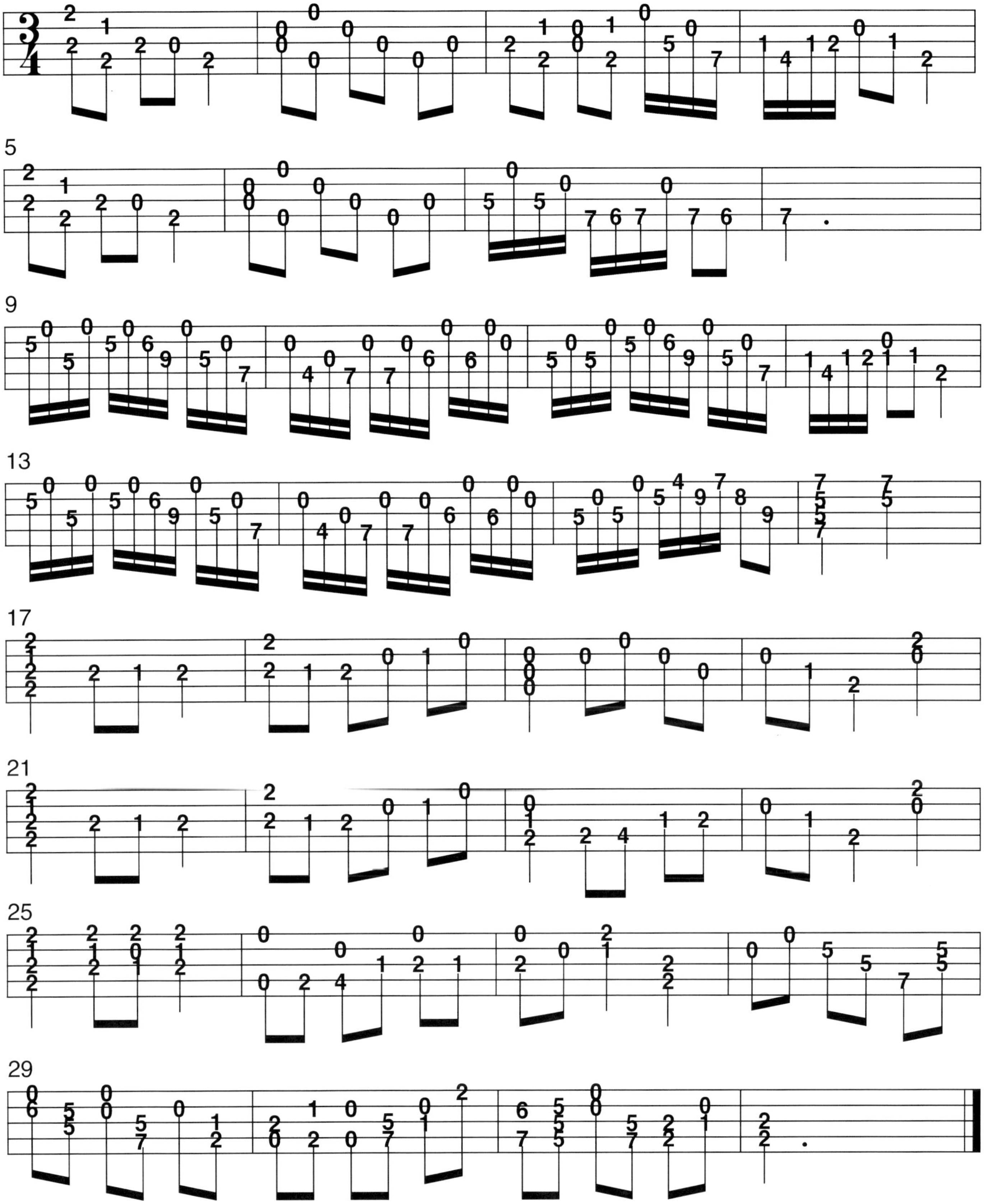

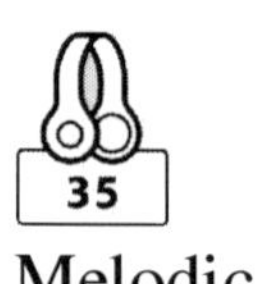

Guardame Las Vacas

A minor

Louis de Narvaez
(Spanish)

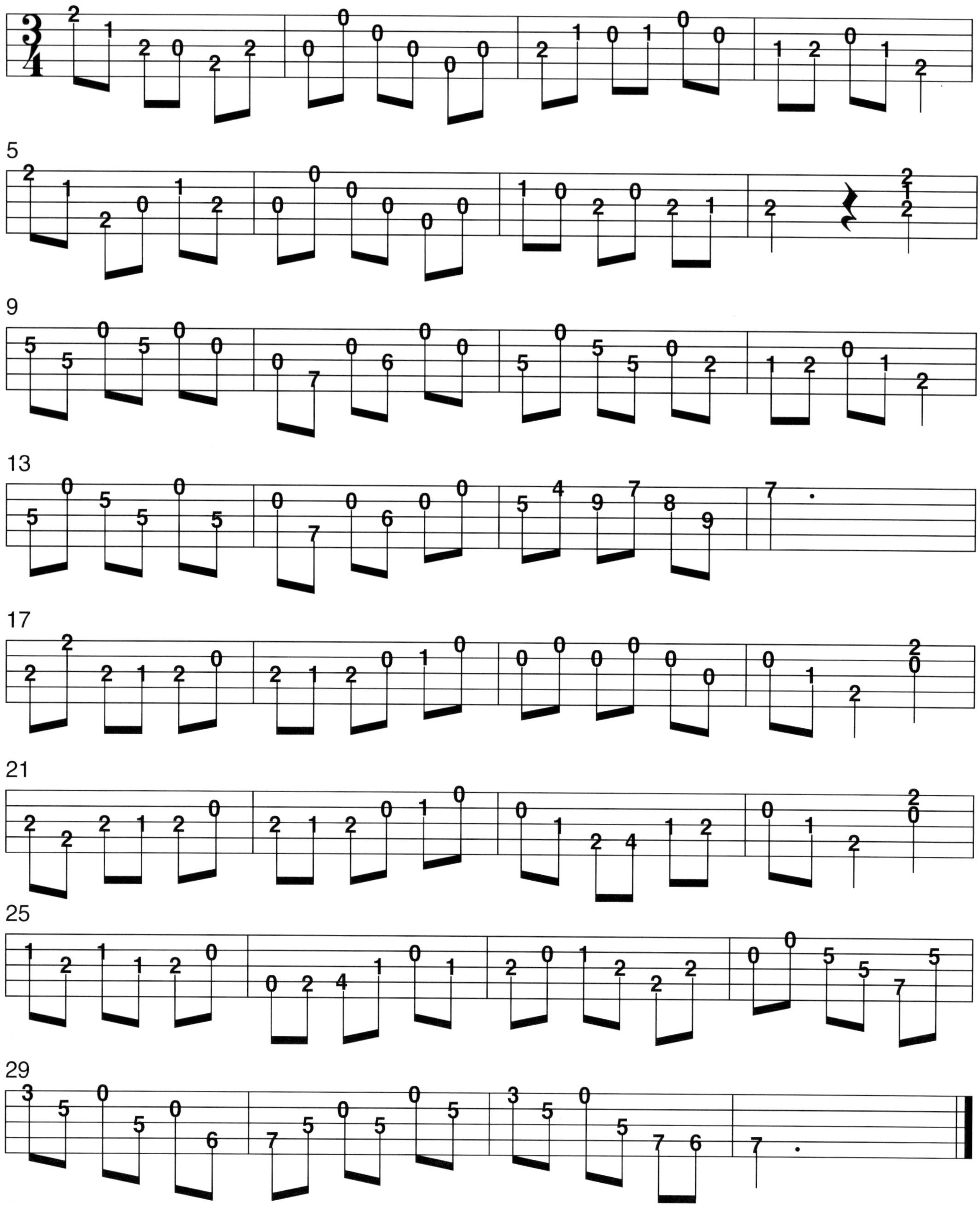

Melodic

Enriquez de Valderrabano
Sonnet (Spanish)

This Sonnet is a thorough-composed piece which is done in a very straight-forward manner. Harmony is kept simple and the rhythm is very block-like in form using strummed or pinched half-notes. Occasionally the 8th-note runs are used simply to break the monotony.

The piece has the feeling that it wants to go somewhere, arrives there, but yet is really unsure whether it really wants to be there once it arrives. This concept can be seen where it reaches a high A note in the second measure but falls away from it. It again reaches a high A note in the fifth measure as part of an A Major chord.

The feeling at this point is that it is happy to be there and will thus remain, but then the following measures see it departing once more. In measures #9-12 it gradually falls away from its former lofty position and descends to a low A Major chord in measure #12. But then with little effort it ascends rapidly and haphazardly to a high A note again two measures later. Then an interesting thing happens.

Apparently since this objective, the high A note, was achieved very easily four times within a fourteen measure time frame, it is no longer desirable and thus in the following measures new objectives are suggested. In the sixteenth measures the D note is tried; in the eighteenth measure it is the B note. But the tune is content with neither and so in the twentieth measure it is the entire D Major chord which is tried. This is the same chord from which the tune began and so an unresolved feeling remains. One can sense the frustration and the tune tries to escape this by falling into a descending run in measures #21-24. Yet this helps the situation not-at-all for that same frustrating D Major surfaces again in measure #25. Escape is apparently impossible and in unthinking desperation the exact same descending run is tried again in the hope that it would eventually lead elsewhere. This is simply wishful thinking for the end is the same, although the D Major chord is presented in a more subdued manner. The tune ends going nowhere and one senses that it finally had come to terms with this inevitability.

The piece is in D Major and so makes much use of A Major and D Major. E minor is found in the tenth measure where something different was wanting after reaching the objective (the high A note) several times. The only foreign chord present is B minor in the ninth measure where it is used to move into the E minor chord.

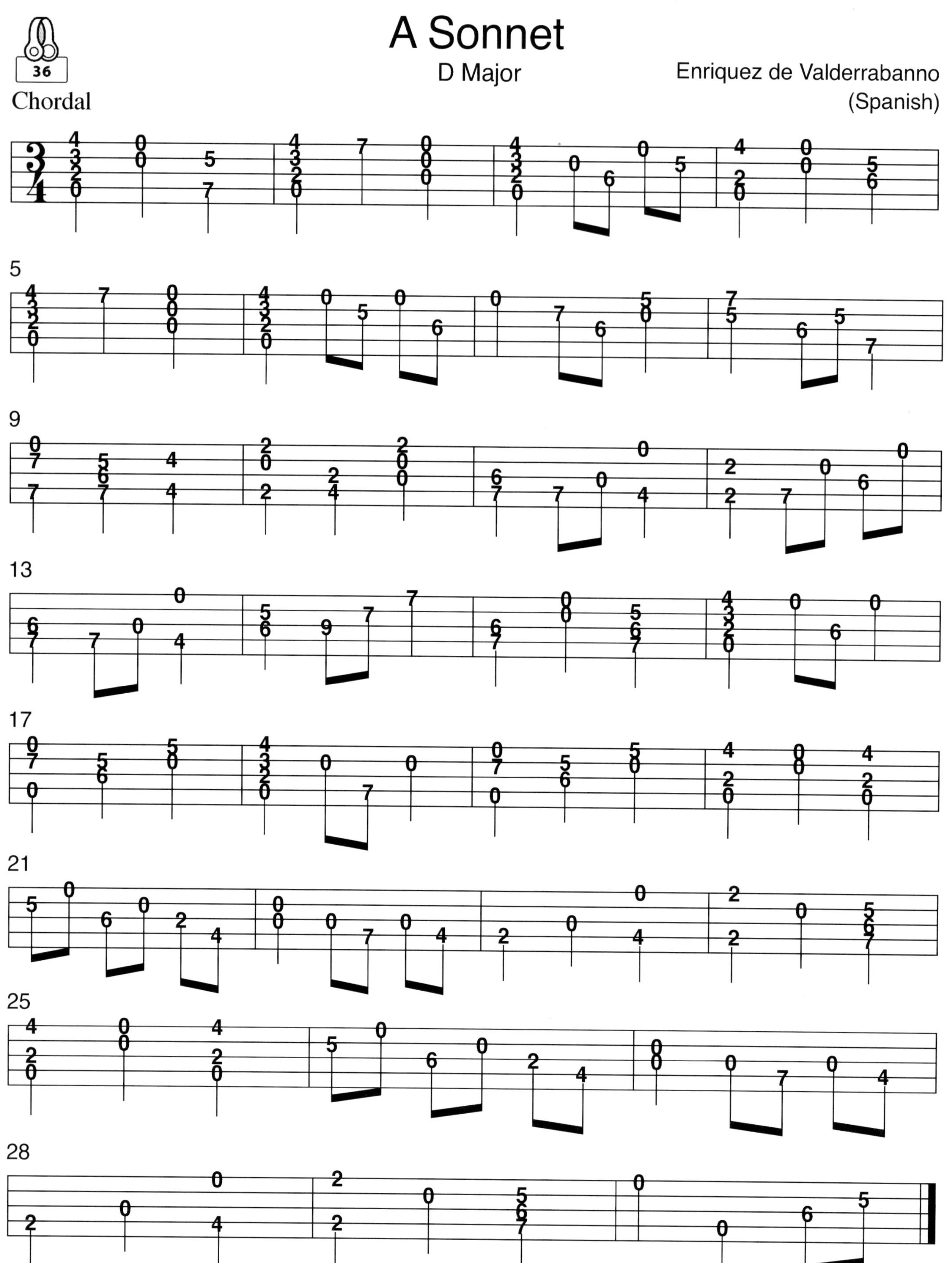
36
Chordal
A Sonnet
D Major
Enriquez de Valderrabanno
(Spanish)

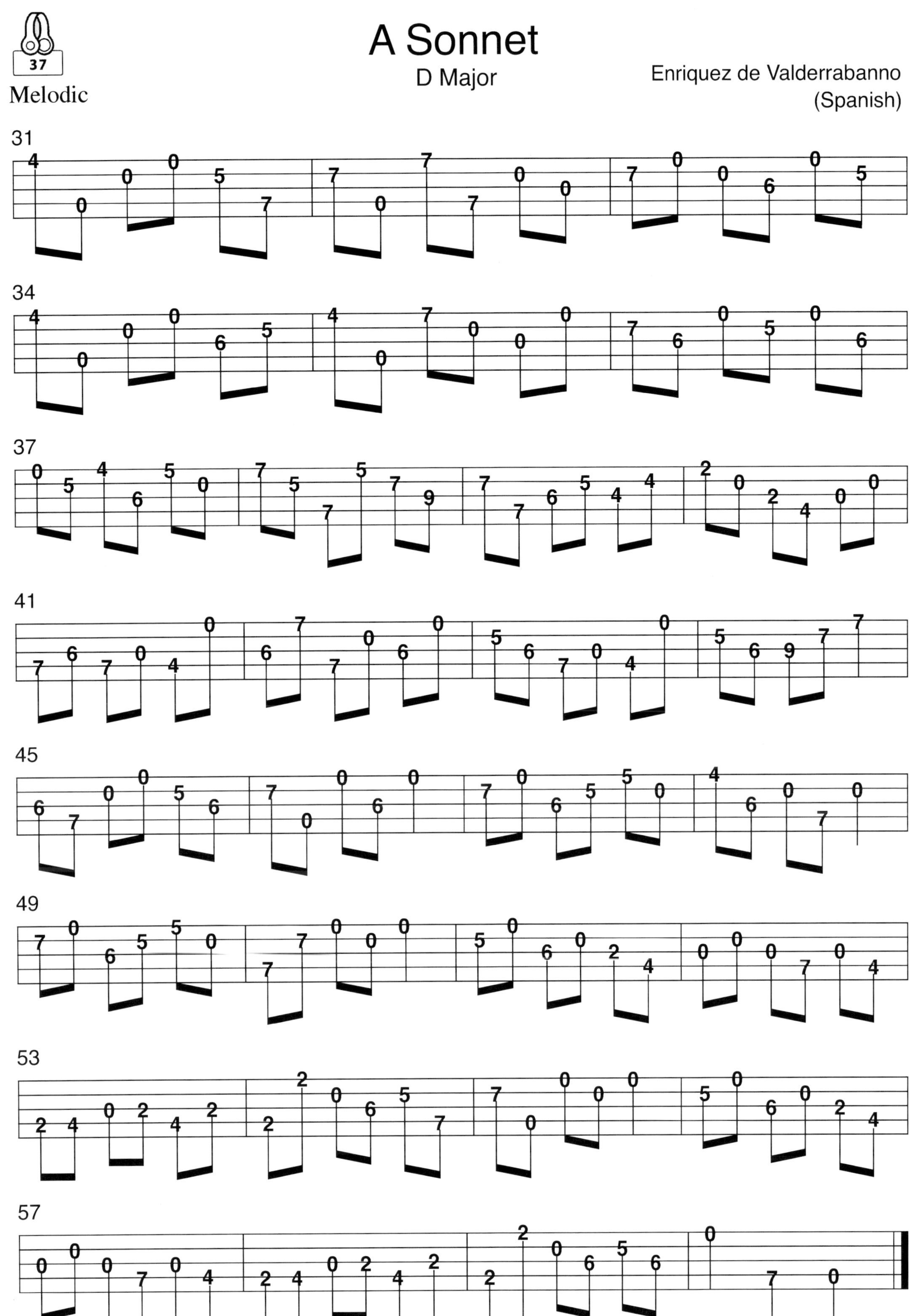
37
Melodic
A Sonnet
D Major
Enriquez de Valderrabanno
(Spanish)

Thoinot Arbeau (1580s)
Pavane-Belle qui Tiens Ma Vie (French)

I learned this lovely tune from an old John Renbourne recording. It can be either a lively dance tempo or a more doubtful treatment complete with vocals. It is strophic and obviously in dance form. Giving to its block-like, vertical character and somber sound it begs to be played as a deathmarch. When attempted to be played as a brisk dance, one feels the tune itself slowing you down.

The work is of the type that begins in a minor key yet ends in the major. It is in E minor throughout and many of the chords seen, such as D Major and C Major, are closely related to its relative major, G Major, which is also used in abundance. This is especially true for the first part. In the second section, A Major shows up surprisingly in the tenth and fourteenth measures, and its relative minor, F♯ minor, appears in measures #11 and #15. B Major is used in these same measures in a very interesting way. In measure #11 it resolves into E minor of measure #12, whereas in measure #15 it transforms into E Major, which happens to be a more common resolution.

Belle qui Tiens Ma Vie

E minor

Thoinot Arbeau
(French)

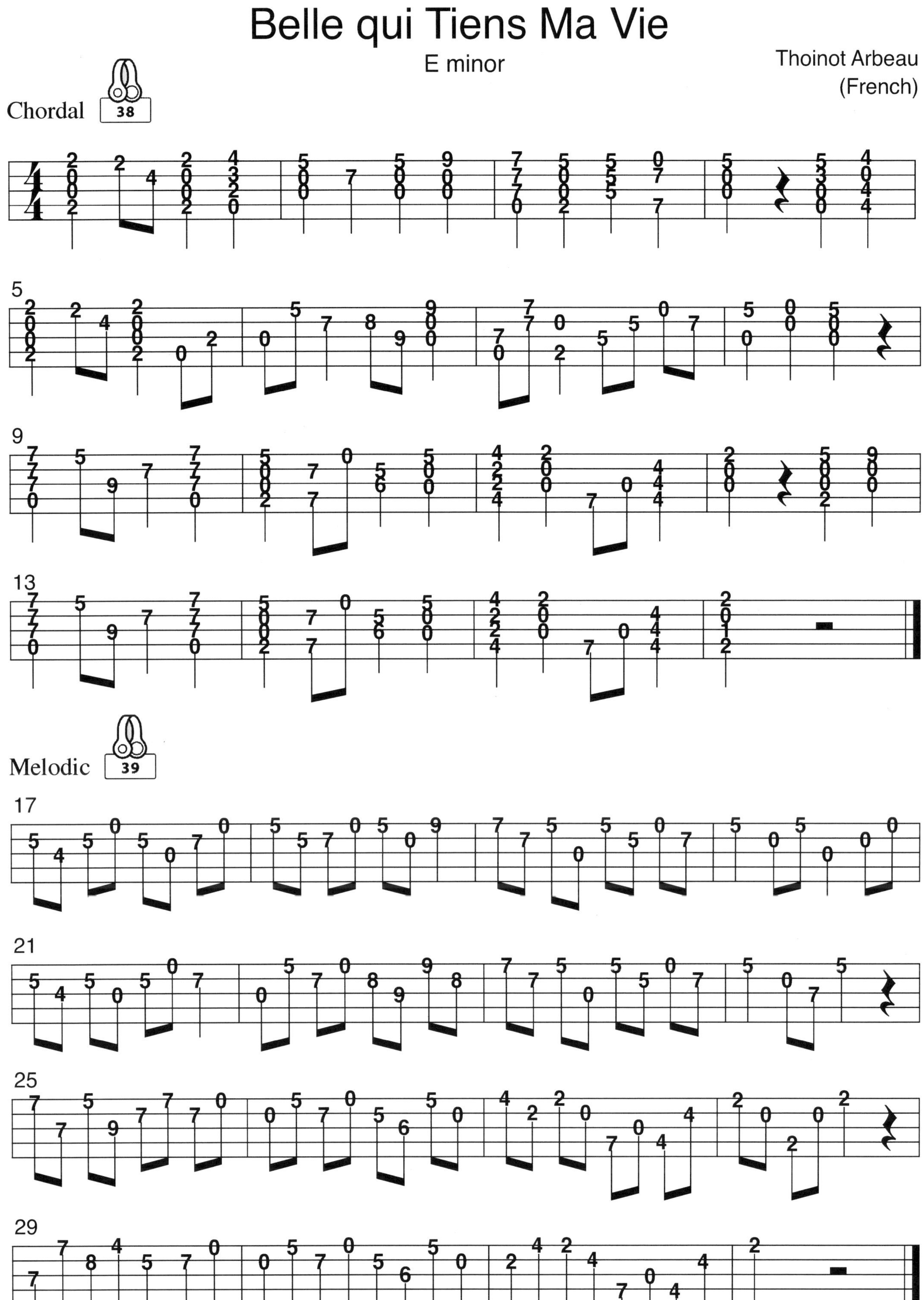

This page has been left blank to avoid awkward page turns.

Jean Baptiste Besarde (1567-1625)
A Galliarde (French)

This is a very simple dance tune which is not in the standard dance form. It is somewhat thorough-composed yet so short and simple in nature that it was labeled a Galliarde. It is a good example of a transitional form of dance. One that is becoming stylized yet its simplicity gives away its folk-like origins. The tune exhibits a common technique in music of the period. This is where a chord is sounded and then immediately followed by another chord identical to the first but a half tone lower. This technique was common throughout Europe but it eventually became passe and then abandoned. It survived principally in Spain. When used it brings to mind bullfights and Mexican banditos. In this piece it is found only once in the sixth and seventh measures where an F Major chord descends immediately to an E Major chord, one-half tone lower.

This piece is yet another one of those that begin with a minor chord but ends with the major of that chord. Here it begins in A minor and ends in A Major. However, most of the work is in A minor for the first two measures and then travels upward to G Major for two more measures and thus ends the phrase in G Major. It returns to A minor and then presents the "Spanish lick." Measures #9-11 are similar to the first two yet here it is C Major which travels up to meet G Major. Measures #13 and 14 are an expanded linear version of the "Spanish lick" in the seventh and eighth measures. The low runs in G Major in measures #3, 4, 11 and 12 seem to suggest an alternate way to look at the ascending A minor runs which immediately preceded them. The chords used are all closely related except for those in the "Spanish" technique.

A Galliarde

A minor

Jean Baptiste Besarde
(French)

40

Chordal

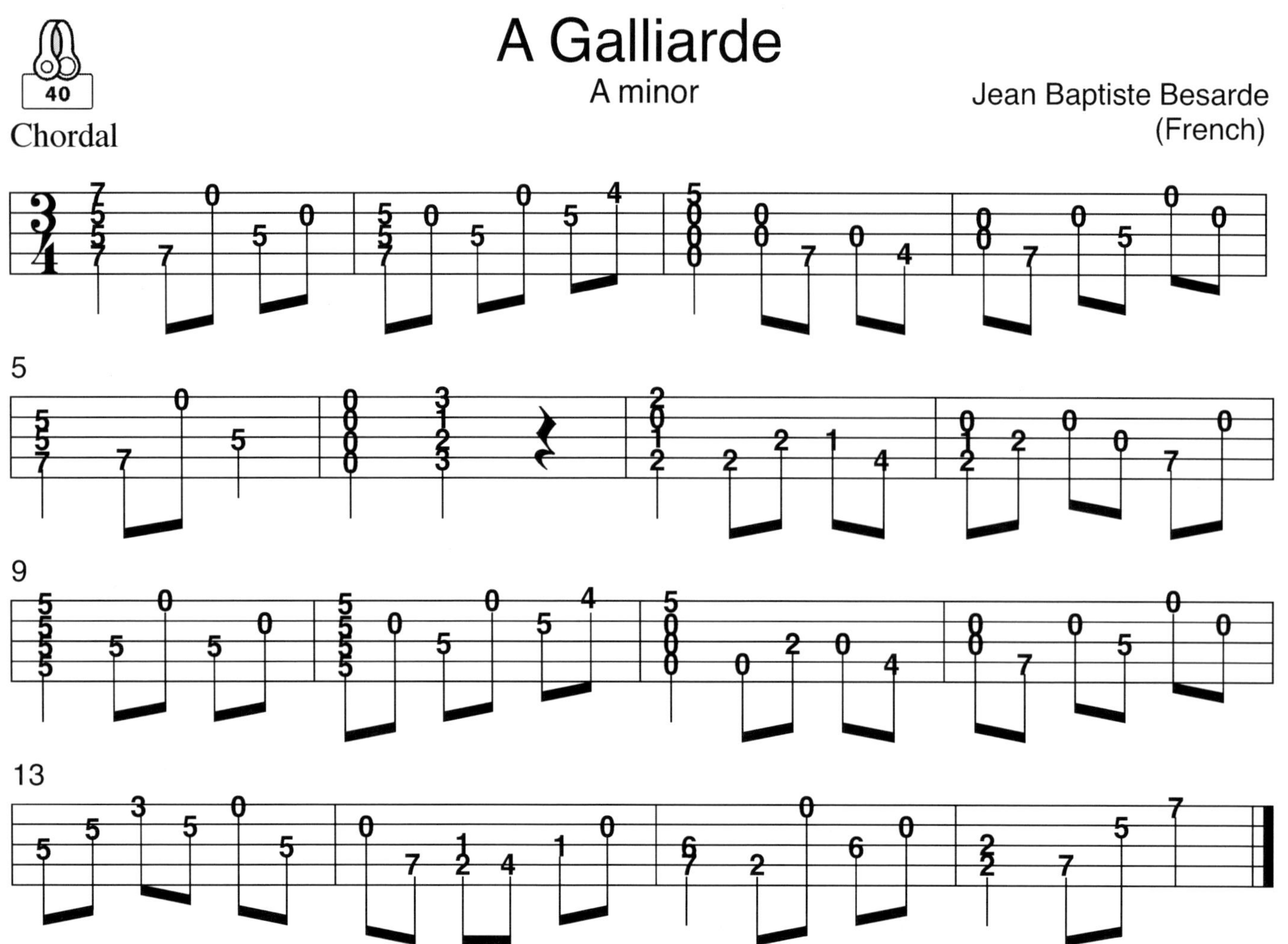

A Galliarde

A minor

Jean Baptiste Besarde
(French)

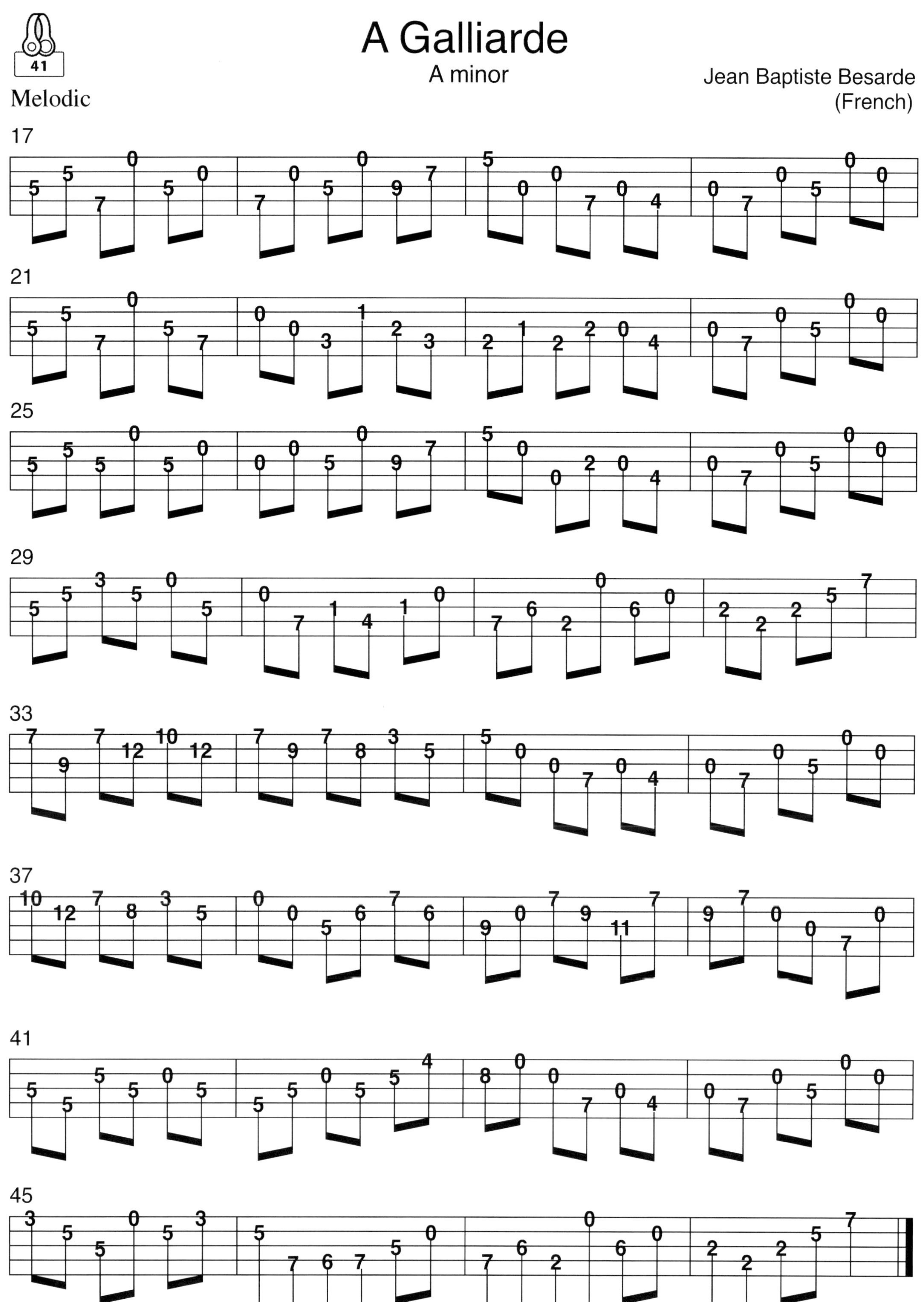

Mirko Caffagni
Etwas Correnten (Swiss)

This is an interesting piece which to many ears sounds very typical of Renaissance music. It is a dance which has an additional section of eight measures tacked on to the usual two sections. This is sometimes found in dance music of the times. Here the third part is very similar to the second. There are a couple of reasons as to why it sounds so typical of the period. One is that it is very modal in character. It also makes use of a device, occasionally heard, where a major chord is stated vertically and then slid down a half-tone. This is evident in the fifth and sixth measures going from an F Major to an E Major chord. This is that "Spanish technique" that was discussed previously.

Perhaps another reason is its overall structure. It fits a pattern which is encountered often. The first and the beginning of the second measures state a rather depressing thought. This then is countered by an optimistic one in the third and fourth measures presumably saying, "but on the other hand." This very same sequence is then stated in the next phrase, measures #5-8, but in a more subtle manner. In measures #9-11 the exact same melancholy message is stated yet it is extended an extra measure, perhaps an indication that now the depression is more severe. But again, as usual, it tries to break free from this in the twelfth and thirteenth measures, fails, and then returns to the melancholy mood again. The very last section will repeat this roller coaster ride of emotions, eventually ending on a dour note as if to say that it was right the very first time.

The piece is predominantly in D minor, yet D Major presents itself rather often. Interestingly, both A minor and A Major are found throughout. E Major is used here to resolve to either one. G Major is seen occasionally. B♭ Major is used to good effect in the opening measure of each section. It is appropriate here for it usually has that lonely sad sound to it when in certain keys – especially D minor. F Major is found in only one spot – in the fifth measure. G6, a very unusual chord, is used as a catalyst in some of the more melancholy runs which gives them a somewhat "empty" sound.

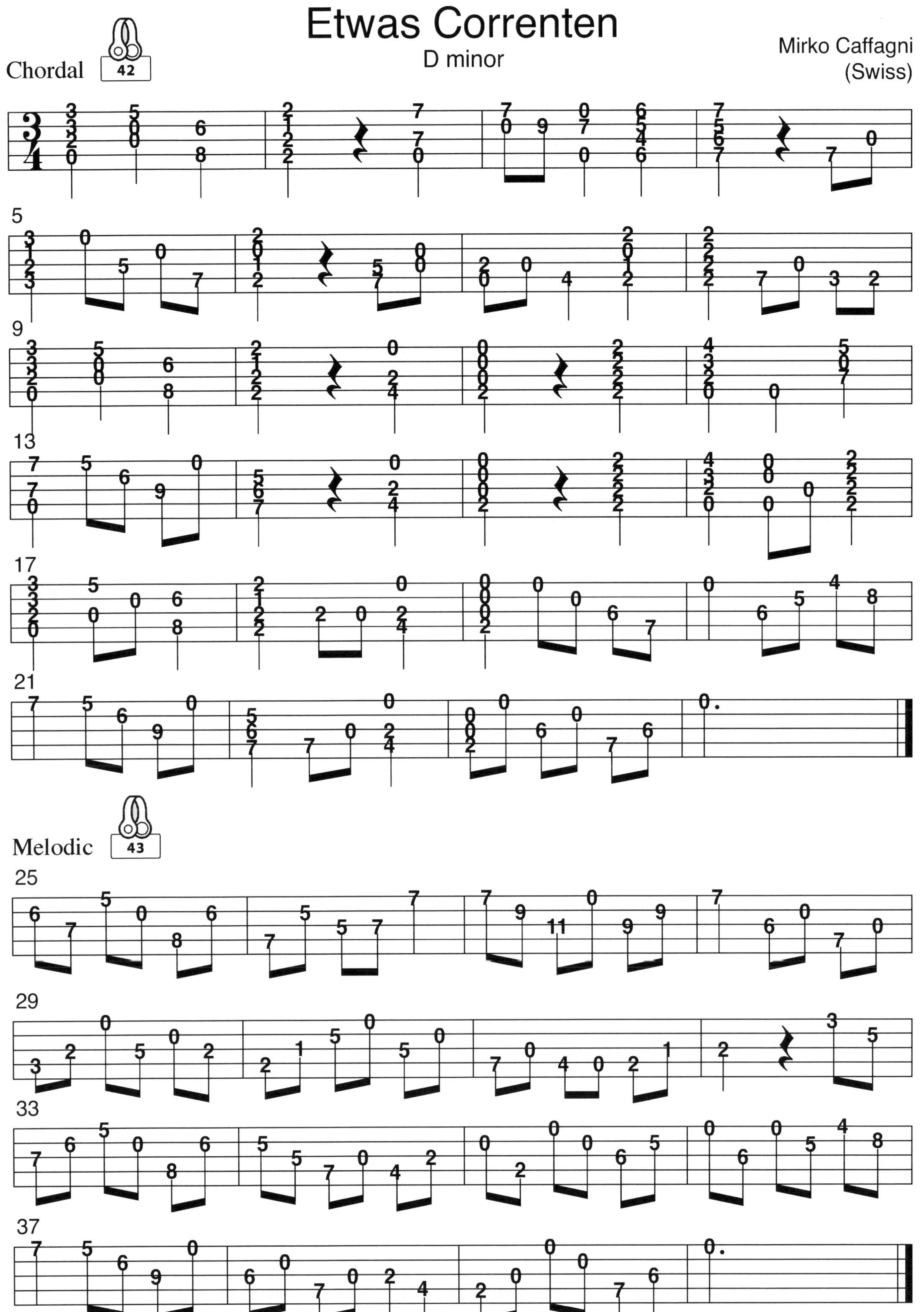
Etwas Correnten
D minor
Mirko Caffagni
(Swiss)
Chordal
42
Melodic
43

Jan Pieterszoon Sweelinck (1562-1621)
Volte (Dutch)

Dutch music of this period is hard to find and so I was very lucky to be able to obtain some pieces by this composer. The works of his, that I possess, all have that mournful, melancholy sound which should be familiar to anyone who works with music of this period. This tune is no exception. It is an interesting piece for a number of reasons. There are twists and turns which keep the performer and listener on guard as well as mood swings, and 16th-note flurries. It is in dance form yet slightly modified for each section is comprised of twelve measures instead of the usual eight. Sometimes one will notice that there are actually two melody lines going on at the same time, which enhances the tune even more. The style is very variable as well. There are vertical block strums, 8th-note melodic runs, and 16th-note flurries.

Like many other pieces of this period, the tune begins mournful, in the first eight measures. Yet within the phrase there are short instances of optimism. The ending of the fourth measure and the beginning of the fifth express this. Likewise, for the seventh and beginning of the eighth. The flurry in the ninth measure seems to be wanting to break away from the depressive low notes which precede it. This is also true of the flurries in measures #11, 18, and 23.

The second section begins on a very cheerful note but this evaporates immediately one measure later and continues on a downward slide until it hits bottom in the 17th and 18th measures. A flurry tries to breathe life into it which succeeds for only a measure as it lapses back into depression for the remainder of the tune. The melancholy of the work is due to the fact that it is a minor key and also because block strums are used at strategic points, as in measures #5, 10, 11, 17, 18 and 23.

The tune is in D minor, which uses A Major and B♭ Major quite often. Both G Major and G minor are encountered occasionally. D Major shows up in measures #2 and 13 while F Major does so in measures #14, 15, 16, 17 and 19. A minor makes a rare debut in measure #21.

A Volte

D minor

Jan Pieterszoon Sweelinck
(Dutch)

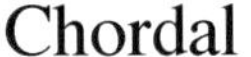

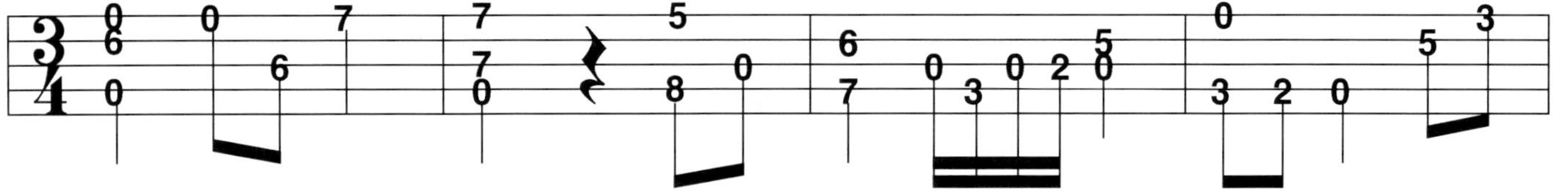

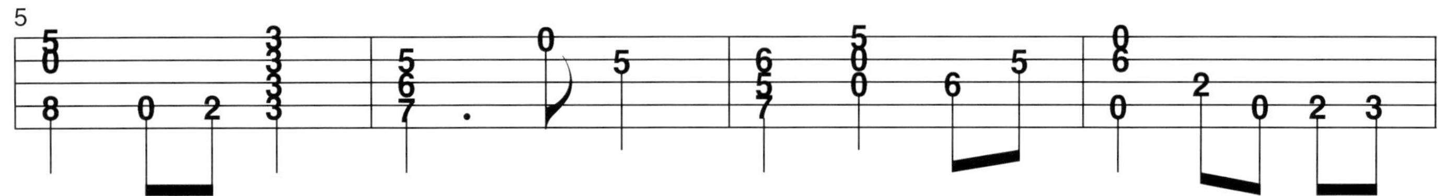

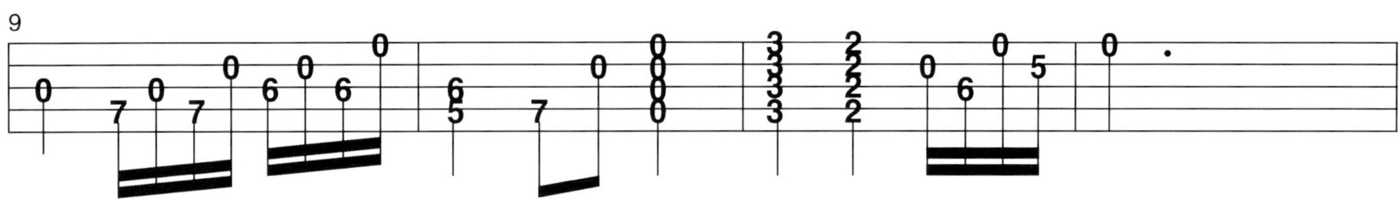

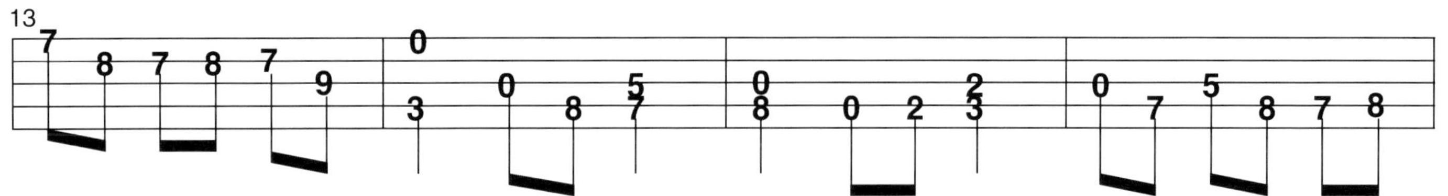

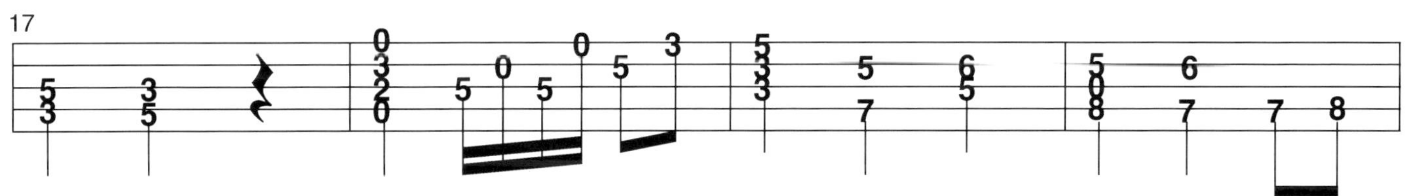

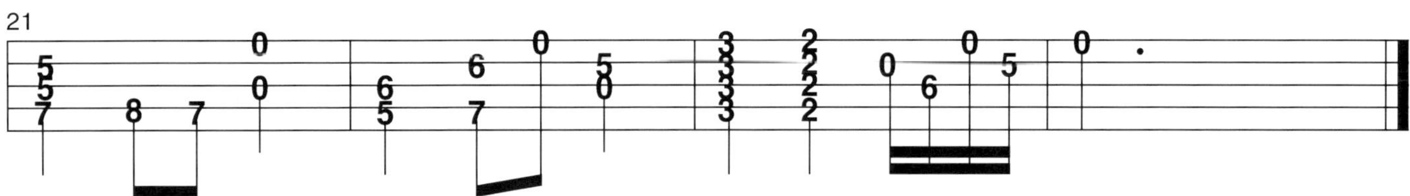

A Volte

D minor

Jan Pieterszoon Sweelinck
(Dutch)

Melodic 44

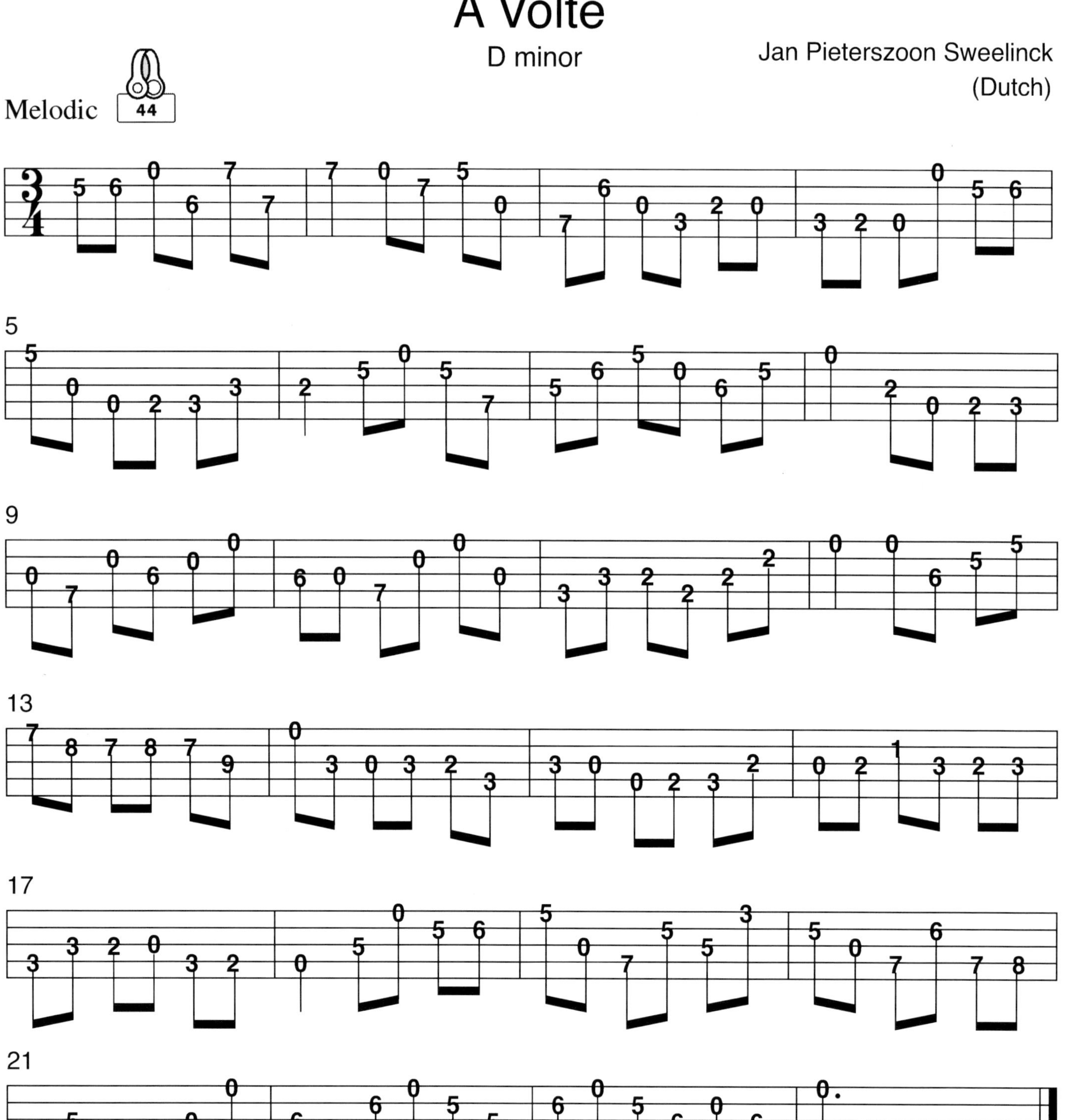

Hans Neusidler (1509-1563)
Ein Nederlandische Tanz
"A Dutch Dance" (Dutch/German)

A very fascinating tune. The reason why central European music sounds somewhat strange to us Americans is probably because we have been sheltered from most of it through the ages. (The exceptions being Polka and the Classical & Romantic era.) When it comes to early music or folk music it is hard to find. When we are finally exposed to it, the sounds are unnecessarily exotic. Similar to Hungarian music, it takes advantage of dynamics and other variations. It uses twists and turns that might startle those not acclimated.

This particular piece was by the most famous Renaissance Germanic composer, Hans Neusidler, labeled, "A Netherland Dance;" it was an imitation of a Dutch dance. It is very dour and has an unmistakable deathmarch feel to it.

Measures #9-12 are rather lively, especially with its profusion of flurries. Yet, this merriment was simply not to be for after the sixteenth measure, the performer would typically repeat the first part, measures #1-8, as an ending. Thus depression reigns in the end, and the Renaissance man is content.

The work is in A Major throughout and so E Major should not surprise us. A good deal of the first part and all of the second part are comprised of these two chords caught in a duel. What probably saves the piece is the way that G Major was woven into this fight throughout the first eight measures. This gives it a very modal, archaic flavor – typical of teutonic music at the time.

Ein Nederlandische Tanz

A Major

Hans Neusidler
(Dutch/German)

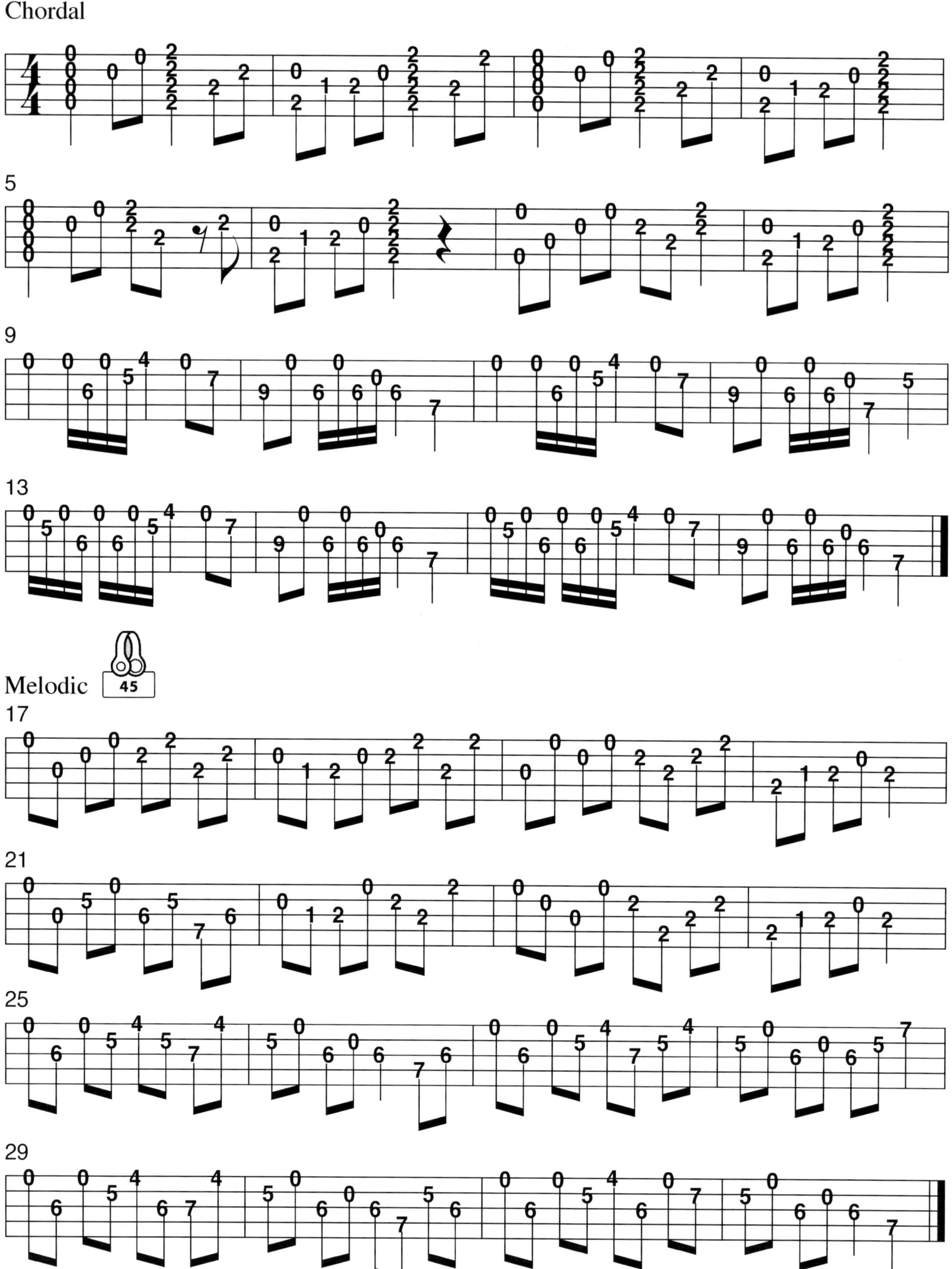

Hans Neusidler (1509-1563)
Lied: Ich Klag den Tag
"Song: I Lament the Day" (German)

"Lied" translated from the German simply means song; in a similar way that "Canzona" translates in Italian. This tune contrasts sharply with much Renaissance music as it is unusually cheerful. It is also structured oddly, but this is to be expected for it is a song and not a dance. It is comprised of two sections, the first of twelve measures and the second of eight. Also somewhat unusual is that the first section begins in D Major and ends in A Major, while the second part begins in B minor and ends in its relative major, D Major, where the piece started originally. These and other interesting quirks are why I am so fond of central European music of this period.

It begins very slow and one feels as if it has a hard time of it. It gradually builds momentum and eventually hits the high spot in the third measure. In the fourth measure it seems to be congratulating itself on its achievement. Having accomplished this it presents the next phrase, measures #5-8, in a complacent noble manner ending it abruptly on a low D note. Measures #9-10 are variations of measures #1-2 and exhibit the same lethargic reluctant quality. This mood is then followed again as in the first phrase by a more optimistic passage. It then falls into depression again in the thirteenth and fourteenth measures. Reflection is shown in the fifteenth measure by the way the D Major chord is presented vertically standing all alone. Complimenting the mood is the F♯ minor chord, also vertical, which follows immediately. It seems to be suggesting another way of looking at the situation – a very favorable tactic when dealing with depression. Perhaps a successful one for the remainder of the song is essentially upbeat.

The work is in D Major and so one encounters A Major consistently. G Major is interspersed throughout. B minor is used here to indicate mood swings and in the cadence in measure #11. F♯ minor is common for it is employed as a catalyst to act between A Major and B minor. It is also used brilliantly in the fifteenth measure to express conflicting thought. E Major is seen in only one spot, the eleventh measure where it serves in the cadence, resolving into A Major. The most puzzling thing about this work is that despite its most unusual cheery feel, the title translates – "I Lament the Day!"

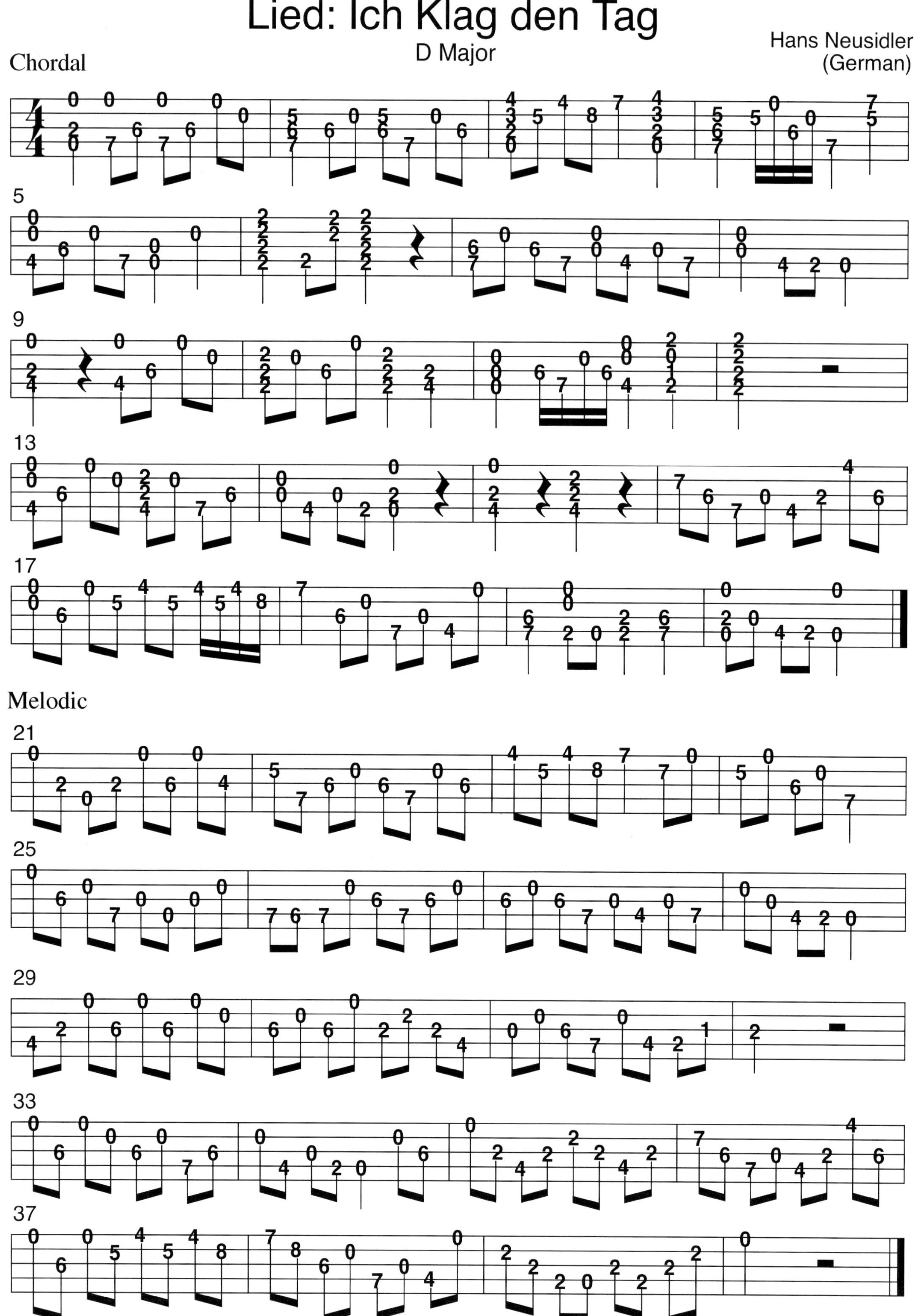
Lied: Ich Klag den Tag
D Major
Hans Neusidler
(German)
Chordal
Melodic

Georg Fuhrmann
Ein Tanz - "A Dance" (German)

Many times during this period a piece may carry a very simple title, such as "a dance" or even given the label "Ohne Uberschrift," a piece without a title. This is probably much more common than most realize. Science and modern civilization has conditioned us to be ardent taxonomists as we seek to classify and pigeonhole everything. The Renaissance man was not so exacting, and thus we find dozens of different names for one tune, and plagiarized plagiarisms.

The work is strophic in one sense, the fact that the main idea is repeatedly repeated, yet one feels it gravitating towards being something thorough-composed. Although it was composed in the 16th century, the style is from an earlier era. This is typical of German areas of that name. Despite being the leader in heavy industry, as far as music goes, she was a stagnant backwater until the 18th century. The melody, harmony, and chordal theory are simple and it has a very march-like character due to its regularity. This is shown in the incessant quarter-note pinches throughout. When these are sometimes broken up by 8th notes, it is done with such precision and regularity that the march is still felt. Examine measures #5-8 and #14-16.

The piece begins with a deathmarch, measures #1-4, but then breaks into a lively, cheerful phrase which will be subsequently repeated a few more times later. This conflict between thesis (measures #1-4) and anti-thesis (measures #5-8) is then repeated supposedly to get the point across. Optimism is tried again in measures #17-18 but this sinks into depression in the following two measures. A short conclusion is implied in measures #21-24. And then again the failing optimism of measures #17-20 is attempted. A final not-so-sunny conclusion in the last four measures ends the piece.

This tune is in D Major throughout so expect the fair share of A Major and G Major. The cheerful phrases, measures #5-8 and #14-16, rock back and forth between D Major and E minor. The fatalistic feeling of the piece is due to the pinched low notes of D Major in measures #2, 10, 20 and 28. There is not even a hint at anything foreign present.

Ein Tanz

D Major

Georg Fuhrmann
(German)

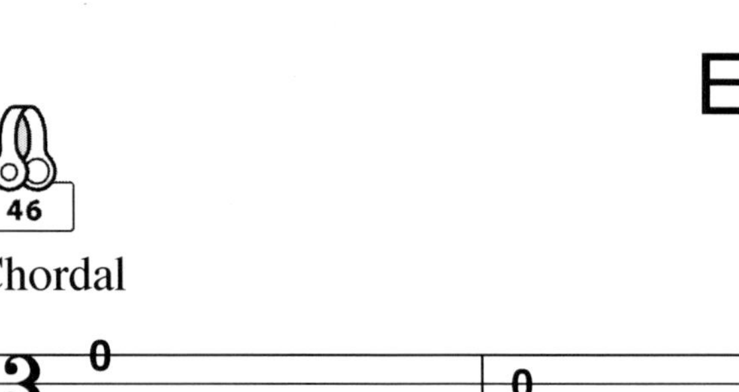

Chordal

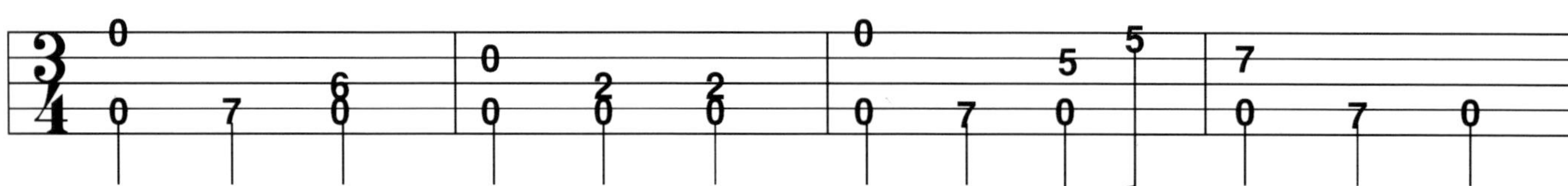

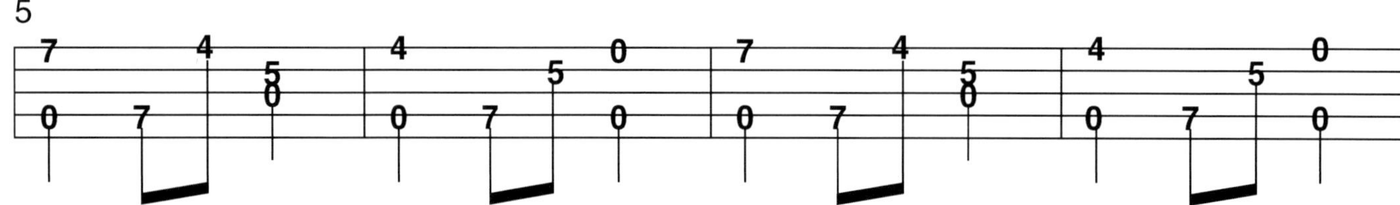

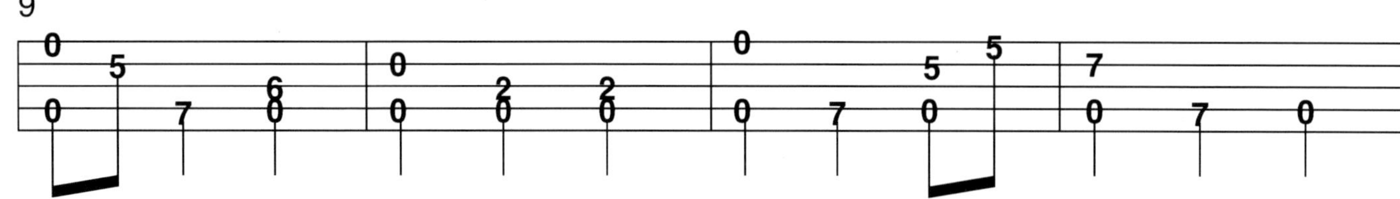

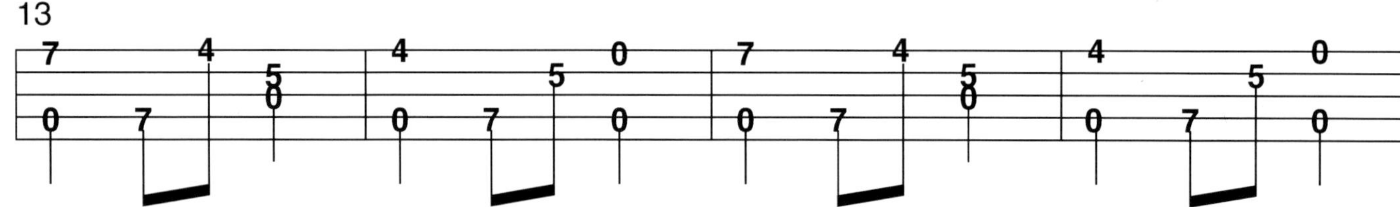

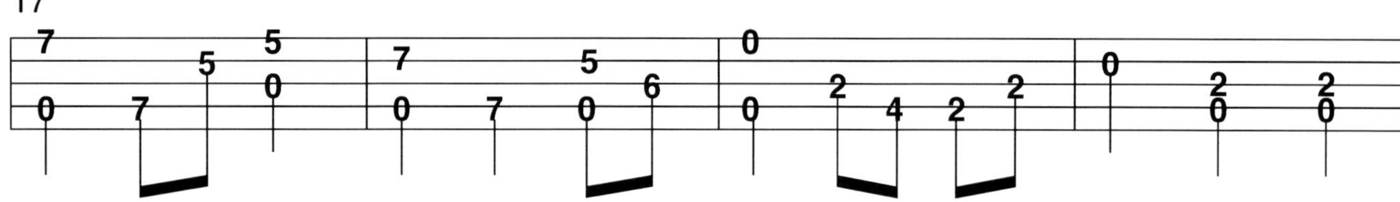

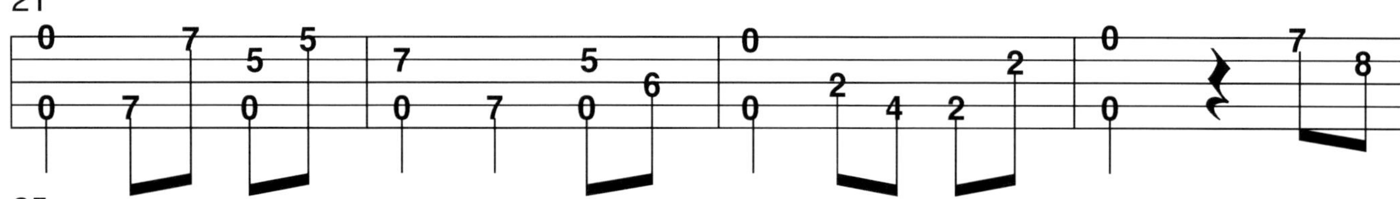

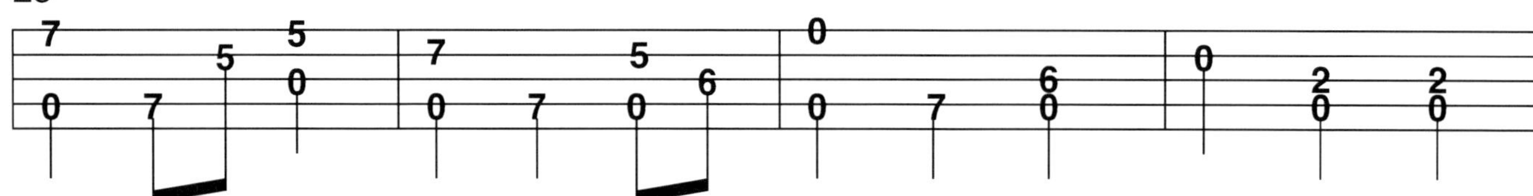

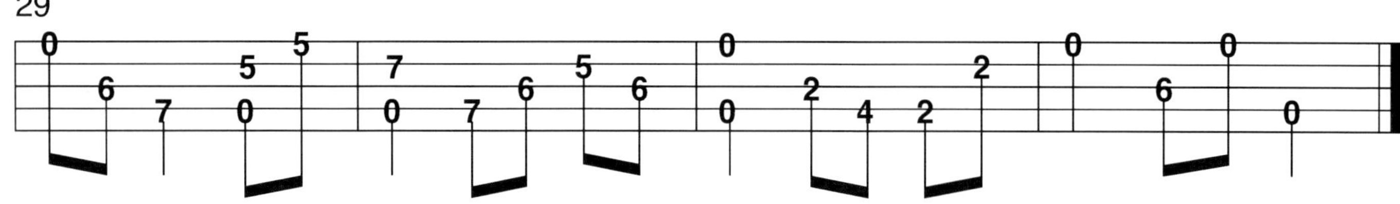

Ein Tanz

D Major

Georg Fuhrmann
(German)

Melodic

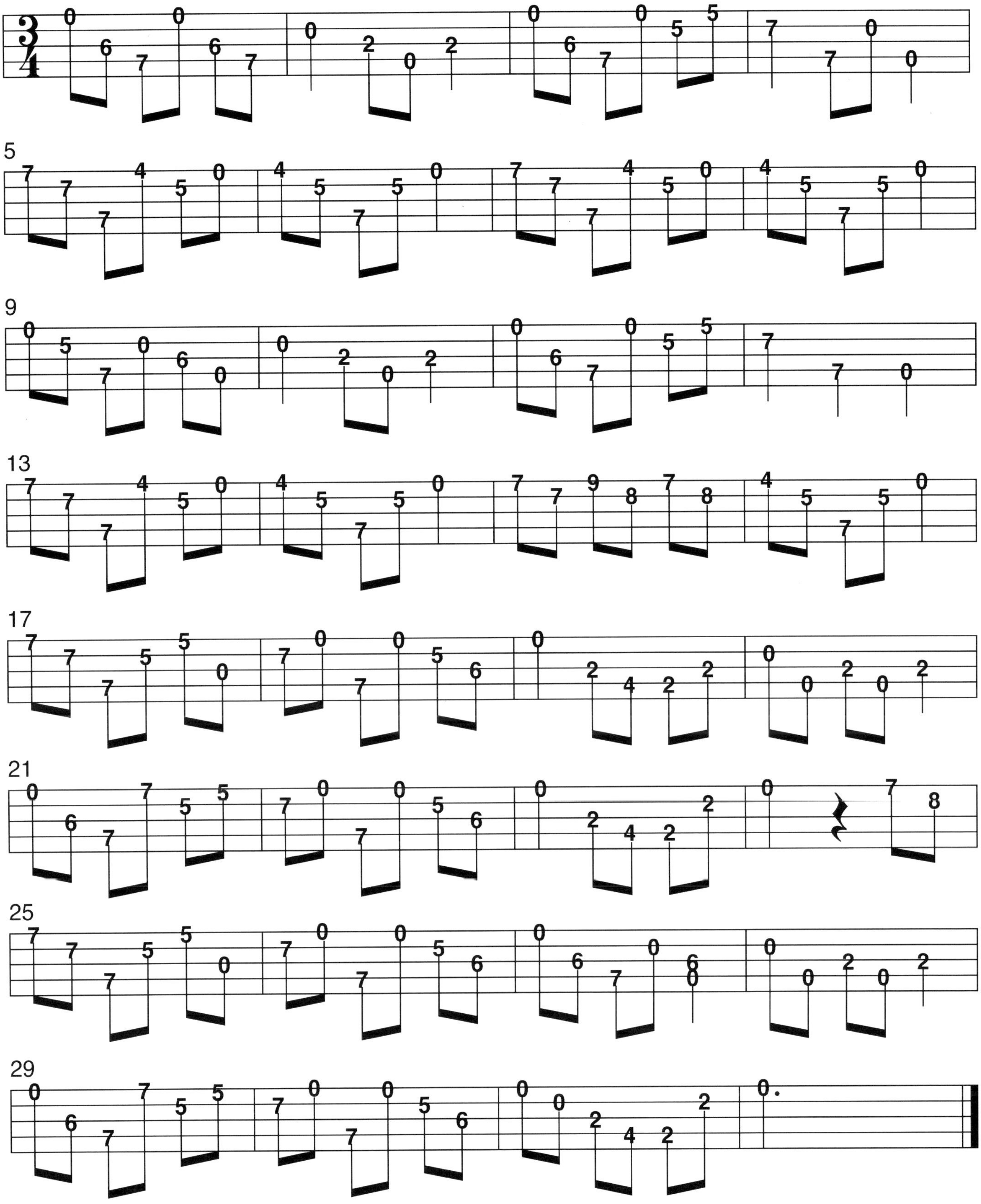

Other Mel Bay Banjo Books